Date Due

PREFACE TO FICTION

ROBERT MORSS LOVETT

PROFESSOR OF ENGLISH   THE UNIVERSITY OF CHICAGO

PREFACE TO FICTION

A DISCUSSION OF GREAT MODERN NOVELS

Essay Index Reprint Series

BOOKS FOR LIBRARIES PRESS, INC.

FREEPORT, NEW YORK

First Published 1931
Reprinted 1968

86325

LIBRARY OF CONGRESS CATALOG CARD NUMBER:

68-16948

CONTENTS

Six chapters of this book are based on lectures delivered under the auspices of the University College of the University of Chicago in the winter of 1930. In transposing them from oral to written form I am indebted for the collaboration of Miss Elizabeth Greenebaum, who has contributed the last chapter.

ROBERT MORSS LOVETT

ONE

INTRODUCTION

THE novel is the form of literature most character-istic, most popular, and most powerful today. It corresponds in our civilization to the epic in the primitive stages of many races, to the drama in the Athens of Pericles or the England of Elizabeth, to the essay in the Age of Queen Anne. It achieved this supremacy in the nineteenth century by lending itself to circulation through-out an immense and widely scattered reading public, by means of subscription libraries and through serial publi-cation in parts at low cost. Though its position today is threatened by the popularity of scientific and biograph-ical works, it still retains its leadership as the literary form in which the majority of readers find entertainment.

The novel is more than a national form; its practice is world wide. Every people has developed it some-what according to its racial characteristics. The examples in the present volume have been chosen to give repre-sentation to masterpieces in the fiction of six nations:

9

the Russian, the Scandinavian, the French, the English, the German, and the American. In each case, however, the book chosen represents a literary type as well as a nation, and has its counterpart, however modified by national differences, in other literatures. All the novels are recent enough to be classed as modern, though two of them are old enough to have influenced more than one generation of writers.

Such a study as this is subject to the drawbacks as well as the advantages of its method. It cannot pretend to be all-inclusive. But with a form as Protean as the novel, no study can be that. And it is hoped that through the examination of special cases, certain general facts concerning the technique, the history, and the function of this tantalizingly elastic art form may be made clear. Since it is essentially popular, the novel should demand of the layman no deeply specialized knowledge. Yet, like all art, it can be better understood, and therefore better enjoyed, on the basis of some acquaintance with its problems and the ways in which they have been met.

Most expository studies start out with a definition of their subject. Books about the novel, however, usually begin with an admission that the subject is almost undefinable. Practically everyone has a vague, unformulated notion of what a novel is, but it is extremely difficult to find a definition which will not rule out some work that obviously should be included.

Time was when to speak of a novel was to imply a love story. But of the eight analyzed in this book, only two recognize love as their dominant theme, and even in these it is somewhat overshadowed. The romantic love theme has suffered greatly at the hands of the realists, particularly since the advent of psycho-analysis. The typical modern novel is not the story of how a man struggles to win his own true love; it is the account of how he struggles to win his own true self. Love is only part of that saga, and so, as the individual is magnified, the love interest tends to be minimized. On the other hand, in such books as *Growth of the Soil* and *Buddenbrooks*, love is played down because the individual is subordinated to the group. Finally, in *Boston*, where the individual seeks his own salvation by losing himself, the love interest is tacitly recognized, although, in writing a propaganda novel, the author does not take time to do much with it. Plot was once a *sine qua non* of the novel, but certain contemporary authors have shown it to be dispensable as was the love interest. In other words, the novel is the anarchist among art forms. It recognizes no law— only the right to give as complete an impression as possible of the world which the author presents through his characters. Perhaps the only safe formula is that it is a long narrative dealing with human (or personified) characters, and that its most permanent attribute is its capacity for change.

One reason for the outstanding popularity of the novel in recent times is doubtless this flexibility of form, by virtue of which it accommodates itself to a great variety of uses and tastes. Modern literature shows a tendency to subordinate form to subject matter. Now the novel, never having been defined by exact rules such as have been laid down at different times for the epic, the drama, or certain types of lyric, was free to adapt itself to all the various requirements of a complex and rapidly expanding civilization. It is, indeed, a secondary form of literature, a hybrid as compared with the epic, lyric, and essay; and it has drawn its elements freely from these primary forms.

In its chief quality as a long narrative dealing with human characters, the novel resembles the epic. In fact, the earliest novels, the so-called Greek romances of the Alexandrian period of Greek letters, were a kind of bastard epic, written in poetic prose, with emphasis upon highly complicated plots and other sensational elements. The novel took over from the drama the important element of "dramatic scene," by which characters are brought together in vivid and natural relations as figures on the stage. It inherited from the romances of chivalry, by way of reaction, the fashion of dealing with the adventures of men in the actual rather than the ideal world, and concerned with satisfying the needs of their physical being. A favorite character was the rascal who roamed through the world, living by his wits, a rogue errant instead of a knight errant. The Spanish word for rogue, *picaro,* gave the name picaresque romance to this type of story—realistic, informal, unmoral.

In England the picaresque motif contributed directly to shaping the novel as we know it today, and offers an illuminating example of the way in which national temperament modifies art forms. The biographical strain in English fiction was strengthened by the interest in notable persons, particularly criminals such as pirates and highwaymen, who were frequently well advertised by trials and executions, and whose adventures formed the subject of prose pamphlets as of ballads. Defoe's novels are, in general, extensions of this practice, and modern English realism can trace its lineage straight back to the writings of Defoe.

When the novel in England was beginning its modern career in the eighteenth century, Addison and Steele had lifted the essay to first place among prose forms.

Some of the English novelists, such as Fielding and Goldsmith, were also essayists, and naturally introduced essays into their novels. Accordingly we find the essay contributing serious or humorous interludes in the English novel down to the present day. Even the lyric has furnished certain features to the novel in the hands of very personal writers like Charlotte Brontë; its influence appearing in apostrophes to the characters, to the reader, or to the divine source of inspiration. Freedom to include at will such various elements has given the novel its eclectic character and its universal appeal.

Because it is so readily responsive to the interests of its public, the novel is always the most contemporary of literary types. For example, one great body of literary subject matter introduced in the late eighteenth century was Nature. The novel, like the poetry of the nineteenth century, makes much use of this material. Scene as an element in fiction, originally used merely to establish a basis of reality for the story, becomes a highly decorative background, and is later given more subtle functions, such as setting the emotional mood of the book, determining its atmosphere, or even implying the philosophy of the writer. Another preoccupation of the early nineteenth century was history, which was regarded as the leading subject of intellectual inquiry. Accordingly we find serious novelists of that period, intent on combining information with entertainment, giving their fiction a historical background. Following the example of Sir Walter Scott in Great Britain, the historical novel achieved popularity throughout Europe. Later in the century, history was displaced by natural science as the chief intellectual pursuit. The novel has clearly reflected this change of background, notably in Flaubert and Zola, and in George Eliot, Thomas Hardy, and Samuel Butler.

The nineteenth century was also concerned with social organization and the relations of social classes, a preoccupation forced upon it by the rapid extension of the industrial system and the progress of democracy. This interest in social reform we find affording one of the serious aspects of English fiction from Dickens to Galsworthy. Occasionally the fictional element is subordinated to the zeal for reform, producing that hybrid of a hybrid form known as the novel of purpose.

The predominance of science in the intellectual life of the later nineteenth century was accompanied by a development of what we call realism in art. Realism may be defined as reliance upon the visible and tangible qualities of the world about us, the things which we see and touch. Just as natural science undertakes to explain the

15

universe in mechanistic terms, so realism has as its object to portray as exactly as possible the external appearance of the small part of the universe that we know. The objective world, which is an accepted convention among rational people, necessarily furnishes the language of communication to all the arts, but in the nineteenth century a more precise and detailed rendering of its phenomena became an aesthetic aim, not only in fiction but also in painting, in sculpture, even in music. One effort which developed in the novel was the attempt to give a strong feeling of real life. As we believe more readily in unpleasant than in pleasant things, the use of the ugly and sordid came to be characteristic of the extreme realist, who, it has been said, tries to mention the unmentionable with as much detail as possible.

Each country developed a type of realism colored by the national temperament. The French group, of whom Flaubert is a type, called themselves naturalists, and the difference between them and the English realists epitomizes the difference in the character of the two nations. In both England and France the rise of modern realism is closely connected with the emergence of the middle class. But the English middle class was Puritan, and to it the legitimate ends of literature were not beauty and pleasure, but truth and doctrine. Hence, in contrast to the scientifically disciplined agnosticism with which naturalism regards all that lies beyond the material world, English realism tends to consider the visible and tangible as possessed of an ulterior significance. Any picture of life it regards as a means to apprehending this significance rather than, with the naturalists, as an end in itself. Thus the spirit of English realism, which is as old as the English novel if one dates it from Defoe, has consistently remained didactic, moralistic, and reformatory.

This philosophical approach is closely bound up with the tendency of English realists to address themselves directly to their audience and to assume responsibility for a personal view of life, resulting in an informality of style quite striking as opposed to the scrupulous detachment cultivated by the French school. English writers have been almost jaunty in their refusal to take seriously the artistic conventions which the French regarded as sacred. This attitude, which antedates the naturalists, has in general persisted even through their heyday. Fielding imperturbably admitted his readers to his difficulties in extricating his heroes from the complications he had contrived for them. Thackeray and Trollope insisted on jesting over the puppet character of the people and events they had concocted. George Eliot approached her task with a program which emphasized the novel as a personal view of life. "My strongest effort is to give a faithful account of men and things as they have mirrored themselves in my mind," she says in *Adam Bede*. "The mirror is doubtless defective; the outlines will sometimes be disturbed, the reflection faint or confused; but I feel as much bound to tell you as precisely as I can what this reflection is, as if I were in the witness box, narrating my experience on oath."

Butler, comfortably within the English tradition, recognized, as did his predecessors, that no human being can be a disinterested spectator of humanity. It will be seen, however, in connection with his novel, that he got around the problem by a device which has proved useful to many of his successors, including so romantic a writer as Joseph Conrad. Since the most recent type of realism exemplified by the "stream-of-consciousness" novel aims at psychological rather than factual verisimilitude, there has developed a group who, while considering themselves realistic if not realists, tend to accept and even to exploit the subjective rather than the objective approach as essential to reality. All this is diametrically opposed to the doctrine of the naturalists, as formulated by the Goncourt brothers in the preface which announced their *Germinie Lacerteux* as a "clinical study of love," and assumed for the novel the responsibilities and duties, as well as the liberty and frankness of science.

The most violent objection to realism as practiced by the naturalists has been based on moral grounds rather than on the claim that scientific notation of life is an illusion. Yet the decline of the technique can hardly be due to the sensitive morality of critics and public since, as Ernest Boyd points out, works which are not avowedly realistic may with impunity emulate the strangest aberrations of those naturalistic books which are condemned on grounds of obscenity. Moreover, both critics and public have become hardy since the days when Zola's own followers rose in a body to decry the crudeness of *La Terre*. The decline of naturalism must be ascribed rather to the inherent weakness of its creed, a weakness which Flaubert avoided (almost in spite of himself) by subordinating science to art, and the English novelists by subordinating both art and science to humanity. That weakness, and the way to convert it into a strength, is suggested by Stevenson's criticism in regard to the limits of realistic art: "So far as literature imitates at all, it imitates not life but speech; not the facts of human destiny but the emphasis and the suppression with which the human actor tells of them."

Naturalism, then, has succumbed to the fallacy of

limiting art to the evidence of the senses, without drawing from this evidence any philosophical conclusions. The demand for some sort of explanation, some meaning in life, is always insistent in the mind of man. Of this demand Levin in *Anna Karénina* offers a marked example. And because of this almost mystical craving, coupled with the inheritance and environment of a scientific age, the two chief requirements of modern fiction have come to be: realism and significance.

The response to the latter demand often takes form in what is called symbolism, which regards the apparent facts as intimations of something beyond and unknown. Symbolism, although a reaction against realism, is also and more profoundly a development of the realistic technique, since selected details seem to acquire an added meaning through realistic presentation. The merging of realism into symbolism will be brought out more fully in connection with *Madame Bovary* and *Buddenbrooks*. For the present it is enough to say that symbolism is to realism as realism is to romanticism: in each case, a new school has carried the hypothesis of its predecessor to a conclusion apparently the antithesis of that predecessor's attitude.

To take the case of romanticism, one thinks of its promulgators as a group who tried to escape from sordid realities either by fleeing into remote times and places, radiant with color and action, or else by withdrawing into solitary communion with nature. But it must be remembered that first of all they stood for revolt against the shackles of convention: for the right of the individual against society, and for the liberty of the artist in the face of artistic traditions governing form and choice of material. The realists accepted their iconoclasm but changed their impulse of escape to one of acceptance, however bitter they might feel toward what they accepted. Thus romanticism really paved the way for realism. As Middleton Murry remarks, "the first conscious and theoretical realists called themselves Romanticists. Prosper Merimée in his famous little essay on Stendhal tells us how even before the 1830's, they insisted on 'what we called in the Romantic jargon of those days *local color.*'" To Stendhal's contemporaries, however, local color signified the color of remote localities, and they cultivated it for its exotic rather than its documentary values. So, too, their iconoclasm had a different flavor from that of the realists they fathered. They concentrated on the grand gesture of rebellion, whereas realism focused attention upon the conditions which produced the romantics' picturesque reaction. Thus the local color idea which had started as a means to romantic escape,

21

developed into the essence of realism, which is a refusal either to escape or to gloss over.

The modern romantic novel began in France with Rousseau, who emphasized the individual returning to nature and flouting society, and in England with Sir Walter Scott, who idealized man into a heroic automaton and hurled him into an orgy of romantic adventure. At present our romantic inclinations take a somewhat different expression. The novel of pure action is still with us, but it has split off from "literature." Detective mysteries, wild west tales, sensational escapades of the African desert rarely figure nowadays among the books that are taken seriously. There is a tendency to bring back the wild west glamour under the guise of biography, (cf. *Billy the Kid*) and to glorify the detective mystery with a veneer of psychology. Much of the current "escape" literature, however, takes the form of humor or sophisticated fantasy. We have learned to laugh at ourselves since the days when Rousseau segregated his Émile from the rest of mankind. In fact it is rather bad form to be serious, and seriousness was the atmosphere of early romanticism. This change of mood is reflected in such fantasies as David Garnett's *Lady into Fox* or Sylvia Warner's *Mr. Fortune's Maggot,* which, although lightly satirical, represent escape through laughter rather than an attempt at correction. But modern romance, whether through action or fun-making, represents a diversion from the main stream of realism which marks the contemporary novel.

There are three important points of view from which this book aims to approach its subject. In the first place, a novel depends on the writer's experience of life, from which his material must be drawn. It reflects his biography. In the second place, any novel of significance will embody something of the intellectual and social interest of the public to which it is addressed; and it may be said that the more fully these interests are developed, the greater the significance of the novel. It is necessary therefore to consider a novel in the light of social history, as belonging to a certain time and place. Finally, the novel is a form of art, the more complex and fascinating for its independence of formal rules.

Of late years much attention has been paid to the aesthetics of novel writing, and essays analyzing the art of fiction have been numerous. Although this method is fruitful for certain purposes, it carries a danger in its tendency to separate manner from matter. In all arts it is true, as one of the greatest modern writers has said, that style (which includes composition and structure) is a question not of technique, but of vision. It is the conception which dictates the technique; and any technical innovation that is not prompted by a conception to which current devices are inadequate becomes cheap and meaningless. In a form as popular and elastic as the novel a separation of the two elements is so artificial as to be misleading. Therefore we shall treat this aspect of fiction, not analytically, but synthetically, through a study of six novels representing distinct types; novels, moreover, which are the expression of distinguished personalities, which associate themselves with certain national backgrounds and portray certain phases of social history, as well as typify certain viewpoints characteristic of our own day.

Growth of the Soil, by the Norwegian Knut Hamsun, is a simple narrative based on the epic theme of man's struggle with nature to make her yield him a home, and as such illustrates the strain of primitivism which has of late made such notable contributions in all fields of art. Tolstoy's *Anna Karénina,* which may be described as a comprehensive chronicle of Russian society, is pragmatic in its philosophy. *Madame Bovary,* the most perfect expression of the naturalistic theory of art in a form most nearly approaching the drama, is characterized by the particular brand of pessimism which was part of the naturalists' legacy to our time. *The Way of All Flesh,*

scientific in its spirit, is an English novel of the biographical type embodying the English philosophy of experience.
Thomas Mann's *Buddenbrooks* gives a picture of
decadence in the type of novel known as genealogical.
And finally, Upton Sinclair's *Boston,* conditioned by
the creed of Socialism, represents the carrying on of a
type which has made a definite place in English fiction—
the novel of purpose, journalistic in its use of contemporary material, and dealing with the social situation
produced by class antagonism.

✕

ANNA KARÉNINA

CRITICS, on the whole, agree that to Tolstoy must be accorded the honor of having written the greatest of all novels, though they differ as to whether it is *War and Peace* or *Anna Karénina* that specifically merits the title. The former deals with many aspects of Russian life during a great period of history; it is amorphous by virtue of its vast scope and weighty material. It is the best example we have of the chronicle novel which follows several threads of events through a certain development in time. The latter, only half as long, possesses enough of this large, diversified character to be given the same classification; but it shows the effect of shaping into a form which approaches that of a series of dramas, parallel to each other, though not bound together in a single plot any more than they would be in actual life.

In one respect, *Anna Karénina* is of superior historical importance. The first Russian work to win great popularity in the Anglo-Saxon world, it initiated that Russian influence on the life of the West, of which Tolstoy was as much the forerunner in the cultural and spiritual sphere as was Peter the Great in the political. Matthew Arnold's essay on *Anna Karénina* introduced not only Tolstoy, but Russian culture to England and America, for Tolstoy opened the way to his contemporaries, Turgeniev and Dostoevsky, and their followers, Chekov, Andreyev, and Gorky, as well as to Russian music, Russian painting, Russian dancing. *Anna Karénina* is thus not only a great novel in its own right, but an important phenomenon in the history of western culture.

Anna Karénina was completed in 1879, when Tolstoy was fifty, and at the turning point in his career. He was born in 1828, and was given the usual education of Russian aristocratic youth. In reaction against the idle life of a young man about town, he went to live for a time among the primitive people of the Caucasus, which was the scene of his first story, *The Cossacks*. Later, as an officer in the Russian army, he served in the siege of Sevastopol, and it was his series of vivid sketches describing this event which made him known in his own country. After the war he married, and settled on his estate of Yasnaja Polyavia, where he devoted himself to his family and his peasants, as he has related in *A Russian Proprietor*, and wrote the great novels which made him famous

27

throughout Europe. Neither military glory nor literary fame, however, satisfied his spiritual hunger for fulfilment of life. In 1882 during a period of general depression and hardship he made a philanthropic expedition to Moscow, of which he has left an account in *What to Do?*

He came to see that the tragedy of civilization is the separation of classes, and further to learn, by personal experience, the inadequacy of mere material relief to bridge the chasm. "It was only when I repented," he wrote, "when I left off considering myself to be a peculiar man, and began to consider myself to be like *all* other men—it was then that my way became clear to me." And that way was "to take no further share in the enslaving of men—to make other men work for me as little as possible, and to work myself as much as possible." In following this rule of life Tolstoy lived, dressed, and worked like a peasant. His writing was directed to proclaiming the need for spiritual regeneration and social reform. It included a powerful play of peasant life, *The Power of Darkness,* the equally powerful story of *The Death of Ivan Ilyitch,* and a novel, *Resurrection,* which expresses his philosophy of repentance and renunciation. In *What Is Art?* he set forth his view that art is not "the manifestation of some mysterious idea of beauty," not "a game in which man lets off the excess of his stored-up energy," not "the production of pleasing objects," but rather "a means of union among men, joining them together in the same feelings."

In Tolstoy's last years he became a prophet of righteousness and wrath, to whom men and women from all the world made pilgrimage. One of these, his young compatriot, Gorky, in a most interesting record of his conversations with the old master, has written the noblest epitaph upon him: "He is great and holy because he is a man—a man seeking God not for himself but for men." In this search, as we must believe, Tolstoy went forth, an old man, alone, to end his pilgrimage at the little railroad station of Astopovo.

Anna Karénina marks the end of the first period of Tolstoy's life. Its main plot follows Anna, wife of an important minister of state, through the dangerous course of her love for the handsome young guardsman, Vronsky. As its background we have a broad canvas of Russian society, beginning with the old provincial aristocracy in Moscow, whither at the opening of the story Anna comes to reconcile her brother, Stepan Arkadyevitch, with his wife, Dolly. She interrupts Vronsky's courtship of Dolly's young sister, Kitty Sherbatskaya, who later marries Levin and shares his responsibilities as a landed proprietor. We thus have four types of the sexual

29

relation: that of Anna and Alexei Karénin, based on a marriage of convenience; that of Anna and Vronsky, based on passion; that of Stepan and Dolly, threatened by Stepan's careless irregularities; and finally, that of Levin and Kitty, which results in a very human marriage. These several strains, brought together by natural means, constitute a large and comprehensive pattern, into which are fitted numerous minor characters and episodes. With his later view of the function of art, Tolstoy was accustomed to disparage this novel as the love story of a guardsman and a society woman. In Anna, however, he has created one of the loveliest and most tragic heroines of fiction, and in Levin's search for the meaning of life and the way of leading it, he has expressed the deepest instinct of his own nature, his truest experience up to the time of what we may call his conversion.

A great novel must have two characteristics, one particular and one universal: truth to the life of selected individuals, and truth to the fundamental meaning of life to all men. It must be both singular and typical, or as we have said before, both real and significant. For the first part of his task Tolstoy had a magnificent equipment. He was a man alive in the fullest sense of the word. His eye and ear were trained to the keenest apprehension of sight and sound. His feeling, excited

by nature or by the appeal of sex, was intense, and his
consciousness alert and penetrating. As an artist he had
a passion for his material, humanity. It began with a
love of himself, his own body. It extended to the men
and women about him, who fixed his eager attention and
absorbed his interest. He records his birth as an artist
in his autobiography, *Childhood and Youth.* His earliest
recollection was of being bathed by his nurse. "I was
for the first time conscious of and admired my young
body, with the ribs that I could trace with my finger,
and the smooth dark tub, the withered hands of the nurse,
and the warm, steaming, circling water, its flashing, and
above all the smooth feeling of the wet ends of the tub
when I passed my hands over them."

This keenness of sensation gave Tolstoy his power of
distinguishing so minutely the physical aspects of the
world and of his fellow beings. No reader of his novels
will need to be reminded of the part which bodily habit,
feature, gesture, and mannerism play in identifying his
characters. Physical actuality draws our attention in the
first pages of *War and Peace,* to the Princess Wolkon-
skaya. "Her pretty little upper lip, faintly darkened
with down, was very short over her teeth, but was all
the more charming when it was lifted, and still more
charming when it was drawn down to meet the lower lip."

In *Anna Karénina* the outward seeming of Alexei Karénin is familiar to us through his melancholy, ironic eyes and his habit of cracking his knuckles. We are never without a sense of the physical effect of Anna herself, full of brightness, vivacity, and charm. The environment is likewise made real, the rural comfort of Levin's home, the sordid provincial hotel whither he goes to find his brother Nicolai on his death bed. Tolstoy shows an equal power of rendering sensation, as when Levin, working with his peasants in the hay field, experiences an extraordinary sense of well-being; or when Vronsky and Karénin meet at Anna's bedside as she is giving birth to Vronsky's child, and three types of human sensitiveness to suffering are exposed.

From his observation of the behavior of his characters, and his sympathy with their sensations, Tolstoy passes to an understanding of their consciousness. The state of mind which Kitty Sherbatskaya, outraged and disappointed by Vronsky's defection, entertains toward Levin, is admirably depicted, as is the mental process of adjustment between them after their marriage. The mind of Karénin is shown when at the races in which Vronsky rides and falls, he learns of Anna's love. Above all there is the masterly study, through the relations of Anna and Vronsky, of Vronsky's discontent with his empty life after he has abandoned his career in the army, and of Anna's morbid jealousy and fear, driving her, in spite of her own clear perception and conscious will, to a nervous exasperation which renders their life together intolerable to both. Finally there is the pathetic confusion of mind and action in which Anna sees the train approaching and throws herself under its wheels, from the railroad platform where she had first met her lover.

In one case Tolstoy makes use of a device akin to extra-realism, or symbolism. In the early days, before Anna has left her husband, Vronsky has a dream: "A little, dirty man with a disheveled beard was stooping down doing something, and all of a sudden he began saying some strange words in French." Later on seeing Anna he learns that she has had the same dream. "And the something turned round, and I saw it was a peasant with a disheveled beard, little and dreadful looking. . . . He was fumbling and kept talking quickly, quickly in French you know: *Il faut le battre, le fer, le broyer, le petrir.*" In the agony of her later life with Vronsky this dream becomes a nightmare to Anna. Then, at the moment when she throws herself beneath the train, she sees "A little *muzhik* . . . working on the railroad, mumbling in his beard."

To turn to the other aspect of the novel, its quality of

33

ingly. I shall always be blaming my wife for what annoys
me, and repenting at once. I shall always feel a certain
barrier between the sanctuary of my inmost soul, and the
souls of others, even my wife's. I shall continue to pray
without being able to explain to myself why, but my
inward life has conquered its liberty. It will be no longer
at the mercy of circumstances; and my whole life, every
moment of my life, will be, not meaningless as before,
but full of deep meaning, which I shall have power to
impress on every action.

✕

Anna Karénina is a novel concerned not only with
individual, but also with national and racial problems.
It was written when constitutional reforms were being
agitated in Russia. Levin's brother, Sergei, is a publicist,
an intellectual. The futility of his existence is contrasted
with Levin's fruitful activity; and in the latter's discontent
with schemes of provincial organization and district
councils, which his brother advocated, we have a hint of
Tolstoy's own impatience with merely legislative reforms
and constitution-making. Social regeneration must begin
in the hearts of men. It is the secret of Jesus which
Tolstoy, like Matthew Arnold, often quoted: "The
kingdom of heaven is within you." These were also the
years when Russia was in the midst of the romantic
movement for freeing all the Slavs from alien rule.

36

The contrast between Vronsky, enlisting among the Pan-Slavic volunteers and throwing his ruined life into the war for freeing the Balkans from Turkey, and Levin's work for his homeland, is quietly brought out in the last meeting between them. Above all, the story is national in its delineation of the Russian landscape, people, city, and peasant life. But it transcends the national in its handling of the universal theme, the life cycle: birth, growth, progress, decay, death, and the renewal of life. It is universal also in its morality, penetrated by human psychology which enforces its thesis with understanding and sympathy. If, like the Greek tragedy, it has recourse to terror, it also purges the mind by compassion.

In another respect *Anna Karénina* is both Russian and universal. It has been noted as a peculiar quality of Russian novels and plays that they do not draw a sharp line between fiction and life. This is seen very clearly in a drama such as Chekov's *Cherry Orchard,* where, instead of our attention being concentrated on a plot or intrigue to which the characters are drawn as to a centre, it is diffused among the interests of the characters as natural beings, and led constantly to the border line where they tend to merge with the world outside the stage. This technique has been called centrifugal, as opposed to the centripetal effect of occidental drama. It prevails in Russian novels also. In *Anna Karénina,* the centripetal force of the intrigue between Anna and Vronsky is offset by the surrounding group of centrifugal characters who carry the interest of the reader beyond the limits of the story, into life itself. This quality of Russian realism distinguishes it from the scientific naturalism of the French, with its analogy to a physiological experiment, and from the concentration on a single biographical experience, characteristic of the English novel.

Middleton Murry ascribes the difference to the fact that realism "is more than a literary method for the Russian; it is the natural expression of the Russian spirit, a mode of his consciousness." This spirit, he explains, is actuated by the hunger for absolutism in a world which it finds itself unable either to judge or to condemn. "And perhaps we have no writer save Shakespeare who has expressed in the sense in which Tolstoy and Dostoyevsky and Chekov express it . . . an attitude of complete acceptance, that is to say, an apprehension of human life as something which in all its manifestations exists in its own right . . . ." This temper, he concludes, "leads directly to realism, but to a realism of a kind which only the exceptional genius of the West can achieve, to a realism tinged neither by protest nor condescension, but animated and inspired by the profound spiritual issues which are inevitable to a contemplation of life so comprehensive and immediate." It is the combination of the spontaneous realistic technique with a conception which goes beyond the manifestations admitted by the creed of realism, which makes certain Russian novels seem actually to offer the "slice of life" that a school of professed naturalists would capture by documentation and statistics.

The chronicle novel naturally lends itself to the centrifugal technique. As an example, *Anna Karénina* may be contrasted with *Madame Bovary,* which is a perfect type of the dramatic, "self-contained" novel. In the latter the chief characters seem isolated from the world, as constituting a special case for experiment or observation. The subordinate people in the story are only the setting; they do not seem closely bound to the principals, nor does their fate seem to be of moment, even to themselves. In *Anna Karénina,* on the contrary, we feel constantly the effect of a peopled world, a vast fabric of human life in which we ourselves, like the principal characters, are strands closely knit into the pattern.

The very fact that in such a novel society plays the part of fate in determining destiny, gives to the characters an importance transcending that of mere *dramatis personae.* Upon their actions hang results infinitely more momentous than the life or death of individuals. There are eternal issues involved. In thus emphasizing the values of human life, rendering it in terms which make it seem more significant than we had thought it to be, *Anna Karénina* fulfils the highest function of art: not merely to represent life, but to enhance it; not merely to interpret it, but to transcend it.

THREE

GROWTH OF THE SOIL

GROWTH OF THE SOIL deals with the elements of fiction in their simplest form. Its fundamental theme is the oldest in human history, man's struggle with nature to force her to yield him a home. It is thus of the epic, indeed the pre-epic type. Two races have been preëminent in their use of the epic motives of man's relation to the forces of nature, typified as gods or giants: the Greek and the Norse. *Growth of the Soil* is of the Norse type, in that it lacks the delicate fancy with which the Greeks embroidered their tales, and is stern, rugged, and essentially realistic.

Although epic in character, *Growth of the Soil* does not, after the manner of the ancient Greek and Norse sagas, deal with divinities and supermen. It is a simple narrative of simple folk in which there is no supernatural manifestation or divine intervention. Everything is accomplished by natural means. The events of the story are neither heroic nor startling; it evolves as

41

naturally as a flower growing or a folk song unfolding its theme. In the end you feel that you have followed, not the adventures of a hero or the escapades of a villain, but the experience of a man, so little differentiated from the lives of countless other men that it seems in a sense to be the fundamental experience of all. Herein lies one reason for the popularity of Hamsun's novel.

It is in keeping, too, with the modern cult of the primitive, the desire of a sophisticated civilization, more and more cut off from the soil, to achieve escape by participating vicariously, through art, in a type of life which it prides itself on having outgrown. The same impulse is felt in painting, notably in the work of Gauguin, in modern music which turns to folk or even barbaric rhythms, and in the drama. This use of the primitive is an exception among the novels of Knut Hamsun, whose other works are apt to deal with eccentric characters and unusual material, appealing to the desire for the strange and incongruous rather than to appreciation of a theme implicit in the history of the human race as a whole. Such books as *Hunger* and *Pan* are marked by an intensity almost neurotic, as opposed to the serene normality of *Growth of the Soil.* *Hunger* probably contains the most autobiographical material, being based on Hamsun's own experience in the United

States, where he underwent great privation and was forced to keep himself from starving by occupations which were distinctly unliterary, except as material for future use. His other novels deal, for the most part, with maladjusted individuals who represent variations rather than the norm of human behavior.

Growth of the Soil, therefore, becomes doubly impressive in its broadly human motivation, dealing with characters as thoroughly attuned to their environment as the beasts of the field. It offers a profound illustration of the paradox of humanism, as pointed out by Joseph Wood Krutch: the fact that those qualities which we term bestial, such as intemperance of all sorts, are in reality human, and not to be found among the animals; whereas those virtues which we exalt as the ornaments of humanity are, in some cases, far more prevalent among the so-called brutes than in civilized society.

Viewing the healthily adjusted peasant as a happy mean between the frustrated urbanite and the beast, Hamsun employs his four great themes—Nature, Love, Birth, and Death—with the simplicity best adapted to his thesis. A fifth theme, common to epics, is but lightly touched upon—that of war. Whatever conflict enters his tale occurs between man and the natural forces which oppose him, rather than between man and man.

Yet even this is struggle purged of the bitterness inherent in warfare, since man is essentially in tune with the very elements against which he strives. That strife is itself but the wholesome conflict which Nietzsche recommends as the basis of friendship.

The themes of Nature, Love, Birth, and Death have furnished material for far more elaborate novels. It is their treatment which determines the quality of this one. The story which embodies them, elementary as it is, depends for its character rather on the emphasis than on the events that compose it. A man settles upon a piece of land, cultivates it, finds a woman, begets children. The complications born of external circumstance and human nature threaten him, but strong with the wisdom of that wider nature which is both his master and his slave, which flows through him as intimately as the blood in his veins, he plows straight on to the end of his furrow, undismayed.

The book opens promptly and properly, by putting Isak in contact with the soil:

✕

The worst of his task had been to find the place; this no man's place, but his. Now, there was work to fill his days. He started at once, stripping birch bark in the woods farther off, while the sap was still in the trees.

The bark he pressed and dried, and when he had gathered a heavy load, carried it all the miles back to the village, to be sold for building. Then back to the hillside, with new sacks of food and implements; flour and pork, a cooking-pot, a spade—out and back along the way he had come, carrying loads all the time. A born carrier of loads, a lumbering barge of a man in the forest—oh, as if he loved his calling, tramping long roads and carrying heavy burdens; as if life without a load upon one's shoulders was a miserable thing, no life for him.

✕

The love theme follows immediately; not the sophisticated love, divorced from all ends save the emotion itself, but the primal impulse which prompts man to mate as the animals mate, for propagation and mutual aid. Birth and death, when they come, are treated as primitively. Very different from the highly wrought tension of such a book as *Anna Karénina* is the scene where Inger without ado lies down to bring forth her child unaided, then rises and, discovering that it has a hare-lip like her own, kills it:

✕

Inger sat down on the door-slab. She was in pain; her face was aflame. She had kept her feet till Isak was gone; now he and the bull were out of sight, and she could give way to a groan without fear. Little Eleseus

45

can talk a little already; he asks: "Mama hurt?"—"Yes, hurt." He mimics her, pressing his hands to his sides and groaning. Little Sivert is asleep.

Inger takes Eleseus inside the house, gives him some things to play with on the floor, and gets into bed herself. Her time has come. She is perfectly conscious all the while, keeps an eye on Eleseus, glances at the clock on the wall to see the time. Never a cry, hardly a movement; the struggle is in her vitals—a burden is loosened and glides from her. Almost at the same moment she hears a strange cry in the bed, a blessed little voice; poor thing, poor little thing . . . . and now she cannot rest, but lifts herself up and looks down. What is it? Her face is grey and blank in a moment, without expression or intelligence; a groan is heard; unnatural, impossible— a choking gasp.

She slips back on the bed. A minute passes; she cannot rest, the little cry down there in the bed grows louder, she raises herself once more, and sees—O God, the direst of all! No mercy, no hope—and this is a girl!

Isak could not have gone more than a couple of miles or so. It was hardly an hour since he had left. In less than ten minutes Inger had born her child and killed it.

✕

This summary treatment is in startling contrast to the solemn emphasis which has been accorded to dissolution ever since Sir Walter Raleigh ended his history with the invocation to "eloquent, just and mighty Death." And just as the primary events which no individual can escape are simplified, so the situations which involve social relations are subdued to the more vital relationship of man and nature. The only institution of organized society which appears is the prison where Inger is sent for the murder of her child. There she is both cultivated and corrupted, returning at last superior in refinement and also superior in her attitude toward the peasants who have not known the subtleties of town life. Yet once more she is swept into the rhythm of her former existence, and what she has learned becomes but an overtone which lends new harmonies to the familiar chant of her life.

Illicit love, which conditioned the whole life of Anna Karénina, figures merely as an incident in the history of Inger, who becomes involved as a consequence of her urban experience. And its natural result, repentance, is correspondingly scaled down to a degree startling in contrast with the serious position this theme occupies in novels of the nineteenth century. The attitude of Isak is much closer to that which the present day, in its effort at emotional naturalism, strives to adopt, than to the Victorian insistence on physical fidelity. Yet whereas in the modern novel extra-marital relations are accepted because of the importance attributed to emotional self-

47

expression, in *Growth of the Soil* infidelity is accepted because here the problem sinks to insignificance.

In all of these developments Hamsun's people differ fundamentally from those involved in such a novel as *Anna Karénina*. Tolstoy's characters are much preoccupied with ultimate ends. Anna agonizes over the moral implications and the social reverberations of her acts. Levin is unable to function happily without the conception of some cosmic plan in which he can find his appointed place. Hamsun's people, on the other hand, are concerned with means rather than ends. Their business is to perform the work at hand, and in merging with its rhythm they find the stability and sense of purpose which individuals of more complicated intellect must seek in philosophical and ethical systems.

The one sophisticated character in the book is Geissler, the great man of the community, product and agent of city-engendered forces. On him is visited the penalty and privilege of metropolitanism. The peasants view with awe his power, born of knowledge and complexity, while he in turn envies their freedom from the conflicts and frustrations of urban life. Such a character might introduce a jarring note, but Geissler is so used that he actually reinforces the prevailing tone. At the same time he is able to serve both as *deus ex machina* and as *raisonneur,* or author's mouth-piece. By this device, which in its simplicity harmonizes with the rest of the book, Hamsun gains the opportunity to make such explicit comments as he is unwilling to intrude in his own person:

✕

"There's you Sellanraa folk, in all this, living there. Field and forest, moors and meadows, and sky and stars— oh 'tis not poor and sparingly counted out, but without measure. . . . You've everything to live for, every- thing to believe in; being born and bringing forth, you are the needful on earth. 'Tis not all that are so, but you are so; needful on earth. 'Tis you that maintain life. Generation to generation, breeding ever anew; and when you die, the new stock goes on. That's the meaning of eternal life. What do you get out of it? An existence innocently and properly set toward all. What do you get out of it? Nothing can put you under orders and lord it over you . . . you've peace and authority and this great kindliness all around."

✕

The manner, like the matter, of *Growth of the Soil* differs sharply from Hamsun's other books, and the English translation by W. W. Worster is remarkably successful in preserving the quality of the original. As is appropriate to the epic nature of the story, the style is lyrical, with no trace of the essay interlude. The rhythms are strong and compelling, the words themselves earthy and substantial, the whole movement as swinging and organic as the word epic would lead one to expect. Thus the style itself becomes as potent in the final effect of the book as the material which it presents, and demonstrates how complete success may be clinched by complete harmony of manner and matter.

It is natural that *Growth of the Soil* should be extremely popular in America. Conquest of the soil, first by capture and then by cultivation, has been until recently the great motive and experience in our history. Our literature bears witness to the importance of this theme, beginning with Cooper's pioneer tales, which followed the moving frontier from New York to beyond the Mississippi in *The Prairie*. Later books dealing with more static and less exciting western life followed, although the boom of '49 and tales of frontier desperadoes kept up the old motif of adventure. Of late, however, Wild West stuff has become material for cheaper novels, and the more authentic "prairie novel" deals with the conquest of the soil by plough. Scandinavia is well represented among these books based on the agricultural development of the United States. John Bojer in *The Emigrants* portrays a whole village migrating to North Dakota, where the original social structure is exactly reproduced, each member taking up his former position—a communal theme very different from the individualism characteristic of native American literature. Rolvaag's *Giants in the Earth* is much in the key of *The Emigrants,* though the author has made public declaration that he wrote it before reading Bojer's book.

One of the real American masterpieces which shows a foreign element digging its way into our soil and our life, is Willa Cather's *My Ántonia,* dealing with a Czech family in Nebraska. Interesting variations of the agricultural motif are Rose Feld's *Heritage,* in which the European peasant's passionate, almost superstitious love of the soil is transferred to New England, and *Toilers of the Hills* by Vardis Fisher, who intensifies the struggle with the elements by placing his scene in the dry farming country of the Northwest, where drought, thirst, and dirt add tragic tension to the conflict. In such a book as Mrs. Cannon's *Red Rust* the primitive theme of Hamsun's book blends with modern social needs, for this is the story of a man's effort to develop the most desirable type of wheat for his fields. To the conflict with impersonal nature is added the struggle with human nature's reluctance to adopt new methods, and the record of a scientific experiment.

This scientific element, significant of the city's invasion

of the country, is a step away from the simple epic type, and betrays some kinship with Zola's *La Terre* and *Fecondité* which employ urban technique upon rural material. In the former he is concerned as a "naturalist" with the sordid side of life among the French peasantry. The latter is designed to plead for an increased birth rate, and adds the characteristics of propaganda novels to those of the naturalists.

To contrast these novels of Zola with *Growth of the Soil, Giants in the Earth, The Emigrants, My Ántonia,* is to be impressed with the fact that this or any type of novel is only in part determined by its material. Its style, its rhythm of characters and events, grow from a conception of life which is partly individual to the author, partly a racial heritage. The gift the epic novel has to offer is a picture of man striving with the elements rather than with other men or with his own turbulent soul, and achieving dignity in proportion to the magnitude of his antagonists. Today it is a more sophisticated expression than in the time when it embodied the experience of those to whom it was addressed, but it will find response as long as cities and the repulsion from them continue to operate. And it will find creators as long as it finds response, even though the loneliest farm of Norway be at last equipped with radio.

52

FOUR

MADAME BOVARY

~~~~~~

IF THERE could exist some Platonic prototype of so varied and elastic a form as the novel, the actual work which it would most resemble is without doubt *Madame Bovary*. Flaubert labored for six years to give his masterpiece those qualities of objectivity, inevitability, and technical perfection which make it the supreme achievement of French naturalism. And by those same qualities he made it also the work which, regardless of schools, stands out as typical of the novel in general. This result would have been even more difficult a little later. Fortunately the years in which *Madame Bovary* was written—1850-56—marked the middle period of French naturalism, when the quantity of realistic detail though great, was still manageable, and before the habit of substantiating fiction by factual documentation had degenerated into a mechanical trick.

But if *Madame Bovary*, like all great novels, was in part the outcome of its time, it was also, again like all great novels, the outcome of its author's experience and temperament. In fact, the influence of Flaubert's environment and heredity on his work is so marked that the story of his own life might have been devised by himself to illustrate his own theories. He was born near Rouen in 1821, the son of a physician well known in that locality. The father's character and calling are reflected in the son's work, little as Dr. Flaubert approved of writing as a career. Dr. Larivière, who enters briefly at the end of *Madame Bovary,* is clearly modeled after the successful and somewhat brusque physician, and is the only character in the book to whom is granted sympathy or dignity. But far more significant than the appearance of a specific character, or even the intrusion of medical material into the body of the work, was the influence of his early surroundings on the fundamental attitudes of Gustave Flaubert. His childhood was spent within the walls of his father's hospital, where he would turn from his favorite reading of Homer, Aeschylus, Virgil, Dante, to the spectacle of human suffering about him, and the sight of medical students jesting and smoking above the cadavers they were about to dissect. Such an environment served to intensify the effects of the larger social environment which produced Taine, Renan, Pasteur —the expanding powers of science, its clash with existing standards, and the resultant efforts to attain a scientific objectivity toward human life and art.

Flaubert's own nature seemed expressly designed to respond to this environment. He came into the world, as another Frenchman remarked of himself, with a wound in his heart. From early youth, as both his correspondence and published writings reveal, he was the thorough cynic, declaring at eighteen that "he despised men too much to wish to do them either good or harm." His lifelong study of mankind and its habits was motivated by cold curiosity rather than fellow feeling; and whatever warmth of enthusiasm he had was for the truths available as artistic material, not for the miserable beings who demonstrated the laws of life. For them and for it, he had nothing but disgust. "It is strange," he wrote, "that I should have been born with so little faith in happiness. When quite young I had a complete presentiment of life. It was like a nauseous kitchen smell coming up through a grating. Before you have touched the food, you realize that it will make you sick."

Such an attitude is not only the basis for realism, but it inclines toward the treatment of life as a matter of physical phenomena rather than spiritual values; an inclination which is in turn the first step toward such a scientific solution as the naturalists sought. Yet neither cynicism as a philosophical, nor naturalism as an aesthetic, tenet is incompatible with a strain of romanticism, and this Flaubert possessed to a marked degree. One side of his nature reveled in the grotesque, the mysterious, the colossal. In *Salammbô* the story of Hannibal's sister, he indulged himself in the choice of romantic material and he continued to alternate realistic and romantic subject matter, following *Salammbô* with *L'Education Sentimentale,* which in turn was followed by *La Tentation de St. Antoine.* But even in writing of ancient Carthage he treated it as a realist, evoking through stupendous research the milieu and events with which he proceeded to deal in deliberately sober mood.

His attempt to achieve scientific detachment and well ordered lucidity in his writing was possibly aided by the limitations of his actual experience. For overabundance of material is the great danger of the realist, who runs a continual risk of being swamped under its mass. The one really romantic adventure of Flaubert's life was his grand tour of the East in 1849, which later bore fruit in *Salammbô.* Otherwise he led a quiet, uneventful existence, enriched by his early relationship with Louise Colet, his later intimacy with the literary coterie in Paris, and his famous friendship with George Sand. Visits to her country estate and occasional trips to Paris were the only interruptions in his later life, which was spent on his own inherited estate near Rouen.

Madame Bovary was his first novel and his masterpiece. It was immediately recognized as an outstanding expression of naturalism, bound to exercise a powerful influence on the art of fiction. Its publication was greeted with much the same critical excitement as was evoked in our day by James Joyce's *Ulysses*. Decorous as it seems to us now, *Madame Bovary* was the subject of a famous trial, proceedings of which are usually included in French editions of the book. It also established its author as chief of the naturalists, gathering round him Zola, the Goncourts (whose journals are the livelier for his conversation), Daudet, Turgeniev, and Guy de Maupassant. His later visits to Paris, therefore, were made in the rôle of beloved master, a position which did not in the least alter his pessimism, nor prevent him from remaining to the end of his life shy, sensitive, lonely, and somewhat bitter. Flaubert's type of pessimism must, however, be distinguished from the Byronic variety of romantic despair. It was intellectual rather than sentimental, and derived its will to carry on less from the hope of mitigating man's plight, or the zest of crying out aloud over it, than from an insatiable curiosity concerning the antics of a despicable species.

57

In attempting to achieve the scientific impersonality and precision which formed the prime tenets of the naturalist's creed, Flaubert was thrown back upon a method which based its conclusions on behavior rather than on the sort of psychological analysis characteristic of nineteenth century English fiction. Psychology, he believed, should be hidden, for the artist can know only his own mind. Whatever he may call his character, whether "king, courtesan, or honest man," as soon as he attempts to reveal the inner workings of consciousness, he will in fact be exhibiting only himself. Therefore he resorted to a sort of pre-behaviorism, attempting to treat as non-existent whatever could not be manifested to the senses.

His paramount objective in writing was the achievement of that beauty which is bound up in perfection of style and perception of truth. To his favorite disciple, Guy de Maupassant, he addressed many words of admonition on this subject. It was to him that he wrote "talent is long patience," developing the idea that sufficient time and attention to discover what is still unexplored must be devoted to any subject of which one would write well; and furthermore that every object is unique and will render up the secret of its individuality if the requisite pains are expended upon it. Hence the search for the exact word, *le mot juste,* which, with its implications, became the text of Pater's famous essay on style and, indeed, a watchword of subsequent literary criticism.

In Flaubert's opinion rhythm was as important as words, and he labored painfully to achieve perfect cadence, not only in language, but also in action. This rhythm of event, flowing in what seems an unalterable course, gives to his novel the sense of inevitability he so desired— a fact which is almost ironic, if one reflects that this element of poetry is largely responsible for achieving the effect of a scientific experiment.

The action of *Madame Bovary* starts moderately enough with the introduction of Charles Bovary, good hearted but utterly stupid, an account of his medical education and first marriage. When his first wife dies, he marries Emma, and from this time on she takes the center of the stage. Exasperated by the meanness of her surroundings, gnawed by romantic yearnings for luxury and excitement, she first seeks relief from passionate boredom in an unavowed love for Léon, the notary's clerk. Then she becomes mistress of a "country gentleman," and when he deserts her, takes Léon as her lover. After this point the tempo accelerates; she becomes enmeshed in debt and double dealing, and finally catapults through financial ruin to suicide.

Rhythm of event is closely related to the poetry of

59

circumstance which Robert Louis Stevenson has defined as romance. Yet with Flaubert it yields precedence to that poetry of character which Stevenson calls drama. Flaubert was essentially a dramatic novelist, and *Madame Bovary* shows all the characteristics of its type, beginning with the limited scene which the dramatic *genre* prescribes. The main action is placed in the little town of Yonville-l'Abbaye, where Dr. Charles Bovary settles down after leaving Tostes. The scene is described at the beginning of Part II, exactly as if it were a stage setting. It offers a perfect example of French naturalism, the qualities of which are emphasized by contrast with a typical English example, such as Hardy's description of Egdon Heath in *The Return of the Native:*—on the one hand, a preoccupation with precise detail, colored only by a cold dislike of the scene; on the other, a sense of vastness and of an immanence, whether beneficent or malicious, animating the visible landscape.

It is made evident that the setting thus described in large measure determines the fate of Emma, whose tragedy lies as much in the drabness of her surroundings as in the poverty of her inner resources. Her one glimpse of the social world at the ball of the Marquis d'Andervilliers seems to indicate that her life would have been far different in Paris, where some sort of external activity would have given an outlet to her morbid romanticism. Her life might not have been better in such an environment, but at least it would have been different. The whole emphasis here is in decided contrast to that of *Anna Karénina,* where one feels that it is the nature of the individual rather than the accident of his environment which shapes his destiny. And this contrast strikes down to the very base of the philosophies which actuated the two writers.

Another dramatic quality which differentiates *Madame Bovary* from Tolstoy's novel lies in the paucity of human background. The cast of characters is small. Few people enter as instruments or influences in the fate of the principals. To be sure, the priest, the nurse, the chemist Homais are sharply sketched, as is the old serving woman, Catherine Leroux, who, like the heroine of Flaubert's story, *Un Coeur Simple,* suggests that the fate of a servant interested him if it did not touch him. But for the most part, removed from the stir and bustle of a peopled world so evident in Tolstoy's and Thackeray's works, Flaubert's characters seem to act out their lives on a stage, untouched by the world about them, undisturbed by the reactions of a community so censorious and gossip-loving as a small French village. There are few ensemble scenes, and these—notably Emma's marriage party and the agricultural meeting of the Seine-Inférieure—are distinctly caricatured as opposed to the unexaggerated realism of the individual sketches. This contrast is particularly evident in the agricultural meeting where the cartoon views of the groups are alternated with close-ups of Emma and Rodolphe, conversing *tête à tête*.

The dearth of ensemble scenes again points to the essential difference between the works of Tolstoy and Flaubert. Where *Anna Karénina* is centrifugal in effect, *Madame Bovary* is decidedly centripetal. The former, radiating outward from its center, seems to flow past the covers which bind it, and merge with the real life that eddies around us. The other, withdrawing into itself, stands apart from the swirl of human existence, a bit of human experience crystallized and separated for purposes of observation from the general stream. *Madame Bovary*, limiting itself to laboratory materials, keeps severely to the case in point. Flaubert has been criticized for his lack of large ideas, and it has been suggested that his concern with detail was a matter of compensation. It is, however, hardly a question to be decided in terms of better or worse. The two books, each peerless of its type, represent of the two authors, the attitudes which each illustrated in his life as clearly as in his work—the outgrowing, social interests of Tolstoy as opposed to Flaubert's secluded, ingrowing ideal of aesthetic perfection and scientific accuracy. Comparison of the two masterpieces involves far more than purely aesthetic principles.

The dramatic character of *Madame Bovary* is further evident in its method of introducing characters. Charles is brought on as an old schoolfellow of the author, in a manner which leads one to expect that the writer will be present throughout, as he is in *The Way of All Flesh*. But Flaubert changes his tactics—perhaps he even changed his mind, but did not wish to abandon his first picture. At all events, the presentation is made through observation rather than analysis. Emma is formally introduced with an attendant biography, just as Hardy introduces his heroine in *The Return of the Native*. This method Tolstoy consistently avoids in *Anna Karénina*, which has been thought by some to suffer thereby. Mr. Percy Lubbock objects that since we know nothing of her background we are not sufficiently prepared to accept her falling into her lover's arms.

Having established the character of Emma, as it were by stage direction, her creator proceeds in his almost behavioristic method. Even where he presumes, as he does on occasion, to enter her consciousness, it is usually by means of some physical sensation, as where the scent of the pomade used by Rodolphe recalls to her memory the Marquis' ball. This scent of pomade is but one

63

instance of the rich corroborative detail which forms so large a part of the realist's stock in trade. With Flaubert it remains authentic, even where he brings in matter which at the time he wrote was thought daring:

⚹

Some flies on the table were crawling up the glasses that had been used, and buzzing as they drowned themselves in the dregs of the cider. The daylight that came in by the chimney made velvet of the soot at the back of the fireplace, and touched with blue the cold cinders. Between the window and the hearth Emma was sewing; she wore no fichu; he could see small drops of perspiration on her bare shoulders.

⚹

Heretofore, flies in fiction were restricted to scenes of horror and filth; and desirable ladies did not perspire. The first realists startled their audience into credulity by supplying these hitherto suppressed details. It was left to the imitators to reduce that method to mere quackery, documenting flimsy tales with trivia which were supposed to carry authority on the ground that no one would bother to point them out if they were not true.

In the hands of Flaubert, however, the mere recounting of detail can build up into something significant and revelatory. The culmination of the story, the Emma-

Léon seduction—it would be hard to determine which was the seducer—is a masterful achievement of suggestion, which in itself might have forecast the begetting of symbolism from realism by the mystic element which no art can successfully desert for long. The two meet in the Cathedral of Rouen and enter a carriage, telling the driver to go where he likes, only "On, straight on," forever on and on. We are not allowed to enter with them. Merely by tracing the course of the carriage and the cumulative fatigue and despair of the coachman, the emotional intensity of its occupants is conveyed. More than that, the carriage itself seems to become a symbol, careering through unimaginative streets bearing a load which the inhabitants distrust because it is mysterious, restless, unaccustomed.

From the seduction scene to the end, the story is handled with accelerating pace and increasing skill, until moral and financial ruin crash down together. Flaubert's chronic irony converts the death-bed of Emma to a wry grotesque, showing how the priest and the free thinking chemist Homais—one of Flaubert's most successful minor characters, suggestive of Dickens in his effect of comic relief—wrangle as they keep watch over the corpse. No doubt it delighted the author so to belittle the idea of death. And no doubt it gratified him to add the final

65

twist of horror, which, for all his theories, turned out to be more in the style of that inveterate analyst Henry James than of Poe. For the grieving husband to learn the truth about his wife, and therefore to sink from mediocrity to degradation, was the end most in keeping with Flaubert's estimate of human merits and poten·tialities.

Madame Bovary represents more than a consummate example of the novelist's craft. Emma herself, although presented in terms of absolute realism, may be accepted as a satire on the sentimental romanticist. One feels that in his unsparing portrait of her Flaubert was also castigating his own romantic inclinations, which he constantly disciplined with a puritanical zeal quite at odds with his creed of amorality. Thanks to that discipline he succeeded in limiting the romanticism to his heroine, and preserving for himself the lucid, logical, and dispassionate temper he approved. For this reason his masterpiece typifies what we consider to be the Gallic point of view. Its influence and importance are partly due to this quality of national representation, without which neither the technique nor the naturalistic credo could have been made so potent—and which, indeed, is the *raison d'être* for both.

Among the English writers to fall under the triune

spell of viewpoint, technique, and creed, were George Moore, especially in his earlier work, *A Mummer's Wife* and *Esther Waters,* and W. L. George, particularly in *A Bed of Roses.* The French accent has been modified by the English tradition in Hardy and Bennett. Yet the fundamental impetus has continued and indeed has grown stronger since behavioristic doctrine reinforced the naturalistic theories. In America one of the outstanding literary followers of Flaubert is Theodore Dreiser, despite his sprawling construction and cumbersome style, which tend to obscure the family resemblance. In his aesthetic theories, his use of involuntary memories, his "attempt to set time to music," Flaubert was recognized as a forerunner by so dissimilar an artist as Marcel Proust. As a matter of fact, within and to a large extent outside the group which *Madame Bovary* represents, it would be difficult to find any contemporary novel of importance which does not directly or indirectly owe something to Flaubert. Even where the philosophy of life is fundamentally different, the attitude toward the art and craft of novel-writing is apt to show the influence of the archrealist who was also a romanticist in spite of himself.

THE WAY OF ALL FLESH

IT IS significant that *The Way of All Flesh*, chosen to represent the biographical novel, should have been written by an Englishman, for no other nation has so vast and impressive a literature of biography, and none has drawn its fiction so unreservedly from this source. The very birth of the English novel was due to the biographies of Newgate prison, which the predecessors of Defoe wrote as a matter of journalism, and from which they easily passed over into fiction. How dominant the biographical type, established by Defoe as the great tradition of English fiction, came to be, is evident from the roll call: *Robinson Crusoe, Tom Jones, Roderick Random, Tristram Shandy, Caleb Williams,* in the eighteenth century; *Pelham, Coningsby, David Copperfield, Jane Eyre, Pendennis, Lavengro, Richard Feverel, Jude the Obscure,* in the nineteenth. *The Way of All Flesh,* coming at the turn of the century (1903), gave new impetus to the type and became the forerunner of a series as characteristic of the early twentieth century as the educational novel was of the late eighteenth. Such novels as Maugham's *Of Human Bondage*, Ervine's *Changing Winds*, Cannan's *Young Earnest*, Beresford's *Jacob Stahl* trilogy, Bennett's *Clayhanger* trilogy, Wells' *New Machiavelli*, Lawrence's *Sons and Lovers*, May Sinclair's *Mary Oliver* deal with the biographical problem presented by Butler in the light of evolution, i. e. the emergence of a personality despite unfavorable factors of heredity and environment. Unlike the French naturalists, Butler and his successors did not regard these forces as absolutely determining the fate of the hero; they admitted an element of free will into the problem. But the influence of both schools was essentially realistic; both insisted on dealing frankly with the facts of life and doing away with the moral taboos and restrictions upon material which had limited the scope of fiction in the nineteenth century.

The impulse to iconoclasm came directly from the French naturalistic school. In *The Way of All Flesh*, however, as in most of its successors, the temper of English fiction has dictated a conception and a technique radically different from that of Zola, Flaubert, and the Goncourts. Butler recognized as clearly as Flaubert the inability of a human mind, biased by its own humanity, to give an impersonal view of the life in which it perforce participates. But he solved the problem by a compromise quite in accord with the English tradition, though more subtle than the method of his predecessors. Without exactly writing in the first person, he introduced his author as a character (Ernest's mentor, Overton) in the story, and allowed this *deus* in *machina* to express for him the apologies due to the reader because the author was also of the species:

✗

Every man's work, whether it be literature or music or picture or architecture or anything else, is always a portrait of himself, and the more he tries to conceal himself the more clearly will his character appear in spite of him. I may very likely be condemning myself, all the time that I am writing this book, for I know that whether I like it or no I am portraying myself more surely than I am portraying any of the characters whom I set before the reader. I am sorry that it is so, but I cannot help it.

✗

As a matter of fact, despite his protestations, he was not sorry at all. On the contrary, he exercises the English prerogative so thoroughly that his novel becomes in effect an essay, through which the author addresses the reader in his own person and for his own purposes, allowing his experience to issue as dramatized philosophy. For *The Way of All Flesh* is to a certain extent autobiographical as well as biographical.

It tells the story of Ernest Pontifex, son of Theobald— a clergyman who managed to be both rigid and flabby— and the sentimentally romantic Christina. From earliest childhood, at home, in school, and in college, Ernest is thwarted and undermined by the bullying and hypocrisy which Butler considers inherent in those institutions. Only after an experience in prison, an unfortunate marriage, severe hardship, and the eventual acquisition (inheritance) of a modest fortune, does Ernest win to independence of the ties which have entangled him. With his final rise to intellectual and spiritual integrity he becomes a significant, though not a popular, author.

The early childhood and schooling of Ernest in a measure parallel the personal history of his creator. Butler himself was brought up in a clerical atmosphere, though probably a more agreeable one than that which surrounded Ernest. He was sent to school at Shrewsbury, which served as model for Roughborough which Ernest attended. Like his hero, he did not begin to write until he had acquired economic security, which he considered the first essential to the good life. But Butler won his own fortune in New South Wales, where besides becoming acquainted with the setting later used in *Erewhon,* he performed experiments in breeding sheep which contributed to his interest in and understanding of current discoveries concerning evolution. It must be emphasized, however, that like his literary god-child, George Bernard Shaw, he finally enlisted under the banner of Lamarck rather than of Darwin. That is, he recognized the will as a factor in the differentiation of species, instead of merely accidental variations—a view which carries vital philosophical as well as biological implications.

On his return to England, Butler was in a position to pursue his interests without thought of remuneration. One of them was writing, and his first published book, *Erewhon,* was also the only one to be successful during his lifetime. It combines an Arcadian strain of idealism with a biting satire on English institutions which places it in the same group with *Gulliver's Travels.* In addition to writing, Butler painted, composed music, and delved into science. Each of these fields he entered as an amateur, an attitude which in his case proved an asset rather than a liability. For into all of his pursuits he carried, in addition to a rare intellectual equipment, the freshness and the zest characteristic of the amateur.

Even in fiction, which he was destined to influence so profoundly, Butler was an amateur, and his novel gained, not only in freedom and vitality, but also in the richness of culture which a student of his keen mind and wide knowledge could afford to lavish on his single work. One reason for his reluctance to publish *The Way of All Flesh* may have been that he considered it amateurish and unfinished. It was written in consultation with a friend, Miss Savage, who criticized each chapter as he completed it. When she died he simply put it aside, so that the end runs off in somewhat fragmentary fashion. No doubt he always intended to finish it, but before his death he consented to having it brought out posthumously.

The mingling of biographical and autobiographical method is reflected in the structure of the novel as a double, or rather, a triple point of view. Part of Ernest's life is recounted by his godfather, Overton, who carefully authenticates his knowledge according to the habit of English novelists, explaining what he has learned from letters, from observation, from discussions with Ernest's aunt Alethea—one of the few attractive characters, and probably modeled after Miss Savage—and from Ernest's own revelations. These last are quoted, providing the second or autobiographical point of view and balancing the mature with the youthful attitude. Occasionally, however, Overton steps out of his rôle as reporter and recorder, into an omniscience that belongs clearly to the real author, giving a third point of view wider than that possible to either of the others.

In addition to the informality characteristic of English fiction, the triple point of view permits a variety of treatment in character portrayal. With the minor characters the method is in general purely behavioristic, as when Overton epitomizes Dr. Skinner of Roughborough, by describing his combination of verbal asceticism and actual indulgence at the table, or forecasts the sadism which Theobald is to display by relating his only childhood impression of that worthy: "Theobald one day beat his nurse and teased her, and when she said she should go away cried out, 'You shan't go away—I'll keep you on purpose to torment you.'" But although conversation and gesture give ample clue to states of mind throughout the book, the novelist is not always satisfied to remain outside of his characters. When he allows himself to penetrate their consciousness and reveal thoughts which no mere observer could fathom, he tacitly admits that Overton is receiving aid from Butler.

The English convention permits an author to frequent the private spaces of his creatures' minds in a way which French naturalism, for all its boldness, would condemn as indecent. George Eliot, Thackeray, Trollope, expose their characters' thoughts without apology and without ado. But Butler's method differs in a way intangible, though easily felt. Particularly is this the case in dealing with Ernest's mother, whose character apparently intrigued him since he was busy about it from her early entrance until her death. Christina is shown as a shallow, romantic woman, with an incorrigible tendency to dramatize any incident in which she may be involved. The way in which the author invades her consciousness and spreads it out almost as a monologue indirectly quoted, anticipates the method which certain contemporary novels have carried to an extreme point. Butler did not develop what we know as the stream-of-consciousness technique. But he avoids the mechanical, abrupt statement, and enters into the thought process in a manner more akin to the method of James Joyce, D. H. Lawrence, May Sinclair, Dorothy Richardson, and Virginia Woolf, than to the writers immediately preceding him.

Another point in which he resembles the modern rather than the Victorian novelists is his presentation of character in evolution. Ernest starts with nothing to commend him, aside from his love for music, except his capacity for change. And change he does, from a maladroit, timid boy into an individual tough-minded enough to satisfy Butler's pragmatic standards, though still soft enough to command credibility and sympathy.

In addition to its importance as an innovation in technique, *The Way of All Flesh* must be reckoned with, both as an ecclesiastical and as an educational novel. Here again it reflects the English tradition which, unlike the American, has profited much by institutions. Our novels dealing with church or school are apt to be trivial and namby-pamby. But, possibly because of the greater age and dignity of these institutions themselves in the older country, a formidable list of English masterpieces center round them. No novel of religious background has presented religious psychology of the evangelical type as subtly as *The Way of All Flesh*, or given more suggestive comment on the conquest of the Anglican church by Anglo-Catholicism. As in Trollope's Barchester novels, this material is so well interwoven with the story of the Pontifex family that the two become one, and the reader has no sense of extraneous information being supplied for purposes of edification or propaganda. The school element is equally well integrated with the narrative. The English novels of school life, beginning with *Tom Brown* and not ending with Alec Waugh's *Loom of Youth* or Shayne Leslie's *The Oppidan,* take either a romantic or a cynical attitude toward Rugby or Winchester or Eton, as the case may be. Needless to say, Butler's is of the second type in his account of Roughborough which completed the ruin of Ernest's personality so effectively begun at home.

In this incorporation of a substantial background *The Way of All Flesh* decidedly transcends *Madame Bovary,* where the characters seem to act against a simple backdrop rather than to move among the three-dimensional edifices that represent organized society. The same disparity may be observed in the cultural atmosphere of the two books. Richness of intellectual background is becoming more and more characteristic of English fiction. Its effect, as well as its cause, is well demonstrated by such a novel as Huxley's *Point Counter-Point,* which is packed with cultural alleviations of a life otherwise painted in terms of deepest gloom. Intellectual and aesthetic activity function as the chief constructive movement, the sole means of escape from despair which a disenchanted generation can envisage.

The young writers who employ a cultural background as an almost unconscious emblem of post-war disenchantment are following in the direction indicated by Butler, and no doubt most of them recognize his influence. Nevertheless, though he was far from being an optimist, in his writing this element bears witness to his enthusiasms rather than to his disillusionment. His notebooks, published after his death, bear witness to the scope of his

77

culture and to his habit of writing down fragments of information or meditation as they occurred to him. All of this material contributes to the interest and the authority of his novel which, as has been pointed out, is in effect a dramatized philosophy.

This philosophy is essentially practical, or, to use the technical term, pragmatic. It anticipates the conclusions of William James, John Dewey, and their school. In its iconoclastic spirit it suggests the plays and prefaces of George Bernard Shaw, who openly avows that many of the ideas he is supposed to have derived from Nietzsche, Ibsen, and more esoteric sources, in reality came from, or at least through, Butler. One result of Butler's pragmatic outlook was his belief in the importance of economic security. Another was his skeptical attitude toward the institution of matrimony. His only sympathy with Theobald is called forth by the intrigues of the Allaby sisters which ended in marrying him to Christina. But this kindly flare died down as soon as wedlock developed into an institution which he regarded with equal distaste —to wit, the family. The theme of family life, sanctified by generations of hypocrisy and cant, has become—in part owing to Butler—one of the most persistent in modern fiction. It was natural that the end of the nineteenth century should have brought into vogue a social consideration of the principles of evolution and heredity which occupied so large a place in contemporary science. From the scientific point of view, Butler saw the problem of English youth as a result of exhausted heredity and overcrowded environment, a finding well born out by the physical breakdown during the Boer War and the present unemployment situation in England. But his more immediate concern was with the evils of family relationships, particularly the violation of children's individuality by the stupidity or viciousness of their parents. Theobald's attack on Ernest's personality may be described as rape; Christina's as seduction. However good the intention, Butler condemned it, since his point of view took account only of results and held the motive to be nothing. Ernest's troubles arose from the false ideas instilled into him by his family, through precept and example, and in their misguided attempts to make him a replica of themselves. The first gleam of hope for him appears when at the lowest ebb of his apparent fortune, emerging from prison ruined and disgraced, he turns his back upon his parents. The fact that his battle is still to be won is indicated by his breaking down after this ordeal and weeping secret tears of contrition.

Remorse, repentance, renunciation, all this moral stock in trade of the Victorians, Butler blows aside as so much chaff. Even the desire for certainty, for some stable basis of orientation in the cosmos, he puts aside as unfeasible, and determines to be content without it. Yet in the very act of overturning the idols which Carlyle and George Eliot had worshipped, he proves himself completely in the line such writers represent. Like his predecessors, and like the successors who owe so deep a debt to him, he has waged war for straight seeing and straight thinking, according to his lights. Because his lights were brighter than most and his thinking clearer, the novel into which he compressed years of study, observations, reflection, has set the pace for a swarm of followers, and today supplies us with a landmark to show the turning point of modern English fiction.

✖

SIX

BUDDENBROOKS

GENEALOGICAL novels, represented by Thomas Mann's *Buddenbrooks,* must be distinguished from the simpler family novels such as *Clarissa Harlowe* or *The Newcomes.* In these, the destiny of the individual hero or heroine is visibly influenced by his membership in a family group which thus assumes a rôle more active than mere background. In the genealogical novel, however, the family itself serves as hero, and its fortunes are followed through several generations. Such a plan is usually dictated by an interest extending beyond personal histories and problems; by a more scientific concern with the principles of environment and heredity, which can be discerned only by observations carried through a cycle of individual lives.

Because of its unusually large canvas, this type of novel requires a particular sort of ability. And because so much of its interest is based on biological and sociological concepts, it is of fairly recent development. One of the best examples is found in the *Small Souls* series by the Dutch author, Louis Couperus, whose novels indicate the current preoccupation with abnormal psychology and the revelations it offers concerning the normal. In Russian literature the book which immediately comes to mind is Gorky's *Decadence*. Several contemporary English novels are of the genealogical type, and several others come very close to it. The outstanding English contribution to this category is Galsworthy's *Forsyte Saga*. This was not originally planned as a genealogical novel, but grew into one long before the author or his public were ready to call a halt. It began as a study of the property sense in an upper-middle-class family; but the last three volumes have been novels of manners, a shift of emphasis which reveals the principle of evolution at work upon John Galsworthy and modern society, as well as on the Forsyte family. *The Matriarch* and *A Deputy Was King*, by G. B. Stern, unite to furnish another example of the English genealogical novel at its best. *The Way of All Flesh* has some claim to be counted one of this *genre* since it deals with four generations of Pontifexes, but its focus is so exclusively upon Ernest that it falls rather under the biographical heading. In this country might be named *Certain People of Importance*, by Kathleen Norris, *The Smiths*, by Janet Fairbank, and Margaret Ayer Barnes' *Years of Grace,* which, though its actual span is not long, covers a period of sharp change through three generations and so may be considered as belonging to the type.

As a matter of fact, *Buddenbrooks* itself covers little more than fifty years, but it brings into prominence four generations of the family whose name supplies its title. It focuses particular attention on the third of these four generations: Tom, Tony, and Christian, of whom Tom is the most important since in him the story of the Buddenbrooks is recapitulated. But Tom is a mere episode in that larger narrative which concerns the gradual dissolution of the family and the dissipation of the wealth acquired by its progenitors.

To describe a novel as a story of decay is to suggest an emphasis on the morbid and unpleasant which is quite apart from the actual tone of Mann's book. The tragedy of dissolution is foreshadowed even in the heyday of Buddenbrook prosperity, but the process is effected in a manner which brings out the beauty inherent in decay, and reminds one that the term decadence implies an increase in refinement and sensibility as well as a decrease in vitality. The very style, even in translation, carries that suggestion of beauty in death which is called elegiac. It is a suggestion always, for in this, his first novel of

importance, published in 1902, Thomas Mann established himself as a craftsman who accomplished his effects
by means so subtle as to seem only a happy accident. He
also established himself as perhaps the foremost contemporary writer of German prose, a position recognized
by the award of the Nobel Prize in 1928.

A novel covering so many years and dealing with so
many characters demands an unusually convincing background. This Mann has supplied in terms of the physical, the social, and the historical. Most of the action
takes place in the little Hanseatic city of Lübeck, and
before the book is finished the reader is comfortably familiar with its geography. One becomes acquainted with
its climate as with its topography—its rain, its snow, its
mist, the occasional burst of sun and heat, are an integrated part of the lives and deaths of the people who move
through its pages. These include not only Buddenbrooks,
but also the numerous families who compose the social
stratification of Lübeck: the aristocratic Krögers, with
whom the Buddenbrooks are intermarried, the upstart
Hagenstroms and Köppens who are *nouveaux riches* and
so inferior to the Langhals and Möllendorpfs. All this
human background is unobtrusive, but it supplies that
social third dimension which adds solidity to *Vanity Fair*,
and even more strikingly to Proust's *A La Recherche du*

Temps Perdu. The same unobtrusive presence of detail achieves the same sense of solidity with regard to the routine of daily life. One knows how the family mansion is furnished, what the characters wear, what they eat. This matter of menus is apt to be prominent in genealogical novels, since the dinner table is a natural gathering place of the family. The *Forsyte Saga* includes a surprising number of meals; and a comparison of the two novels would bear out the statement that perhaps no other typical scene is so helpful in suggesting the atmosphere and *mores* of a group.

The historical events which occur during the course of *Buddenbrooks* creep in as casually but as correctly as the gradual changes in fashion and manners. The Napoleonic epoch is still a lively memory to old Consul Buddenbrook and his contemporaries. The Revolution of '48 furnishes to his son an opportunity for displaying his solid bourgeois courage. To Tony it vouchsafes the slogans of liberalism which she employs long after the event is as remote as the lover who preached them is to her. The Austro-Prussian War brings to Lübeck the benefits of having sided with the winner, but strikes at the Buddenbrooks through their financial interests in Frankfort. The Danish and Franco-German conflicts, however, reach the town chiefly as an echo of distant marching and a painless flare of patriotism. War is thus a significant element in the background of the century.

Against this firm, though lightly indicated background, the more immediate drama of the Buddenbrooks is enacted. The structure of the novel depends on a series of family scenes, beginning with the joyous housewarming at the mansion on Mengstrasse—" 'Such plenty, such elegance! I must say you know how to do things!' " Thus the ill-bred wine merchant, Köppen, proud to be admitted to the gathering, sounds the keynote of the occasion. Years later, the celebration of the family centenary furnishes a companion piece to this introductory group picture. Again the atmosphere is one of prosperity. The family has reached the pinnacle of its worldly position. But Tom, now acting patriarch, already feels within him the symptoms of decay; and during the festivities he is called out to receive a telegram announcing his disastrous failure in a wheat speculation. One feels that his ancestors, who had amassed the fortune which he inherited, would not have speculated; but if they had, they would have won. So the family scenes progress, each marking a step in the rise and fall of the collective hero's career; until at the final gathering, after the death of the last male Buddenbrook, his mother announces her decision to return to her girlhood home in Holland. She is the

first member by marriage to resist the assimilative power
of the clan; and its members are left, convicted and con-
vinced of ruin, to seek in some mystical assurance the
compensation for worldly decline.

Birth and death of necessity bulk large in the chronicles
of a family. But it is significant that the death scenes
are far more elaborated than the births; and that the one
birth which is dwelt upon—that of little Hanno, last of
the line—is in itself the threat of a death temporarily
averted. Because he comes into the world ill equipped
to cope with the life his lusty ancestors had relished, his
birth is really a signal to prepare for the funeral.

Death was one of the great literary values in the nineteenth, as in the seventeenth century. Of late its rôle in
fiction has dwindled. But Thomas Mann himself has
experienced ill health and has been in contact with suffering and death in hospitals and sanatoria, so that it
is natural the shadow of death should brood over much
of his work. It plays a large part in his short stories,
such as *Death in Venice,* and dominates *The Magic
Mountain,* which has for its scene a Swiss sanatorium.
In this book illness, both physical and mental, plays a
far greater part than in *Buddenbrooks* which for all its
study of decadence, is essentially normal.

The death scenes throughout *Buddenbrooks* bear witness to Mann's consummate blending of realism and symbolism, and this is true whether they are taken singly or considered as a progression. For the earlier ones are easily passed over, while with the growing decadence of the family the demise of its members assumes an ever more tragic aspect. It is as if the author placed himself on the very line where the two types of writing merge, so that this book in itself demonstrates how realism may develop into symbolism, how the choice of significant naturalistic detail inevitably suggests a meaning beyond its concrete limits. He has not spared unpleasant physical trivia—the minute odors and sensations which can be made to endow a scene with reality. But neither has he overlooked symbolical values. Part of the horror of Tom's death rises from the fact that he who had been so immaculate in life was borne home to his death-bed coated with mud and slush, his white kid gloves streaked with filth. And when his son Hanno comes to die, we are made to feel that he has succumbed, not to the power of death, but to the weakness of his own grasp on life.

This blend of realism and symbolism makes itself felt in the constant use of physical detail, and of objects that serve almost as stage properties: the Buddenbrook hand, "too short but finely modeled," modified to an almost unearthly delicacy and whiteness in Tom, but still recognizable in Hanno; the leather-bound volume wherein are inscribed the family births, marriages, deaths, and important events as they occur. A reverent perusal of this record impresses upon Tony Buddenbrook the duty to family which must come before her individual happiness; and her submission is registered by inscribing in her own hand, wet with the tears she is weeping, her betrothal to the despised Grünlich. Little Hanno also peruses the book years later, and is moved to rule in, after his own name, the double line which signifies in book-keeping that an account is closed. When rebuked by his father, he stammers: "I thought—I thought—there was nothing else coming." Contrary to Mann's custom, the symbolism here is patent. And it is doubly significant, indicating the end of the family, and also, the commercial element which is inseparable from Buddenbrook history.

This pecuniary motif, developed with such meticulous detail, is a comparatively recent element in fiction. Before Balzac, novelists tended to belittle the fact of money, which in the form of dowries, sudden inheritance, buried treasure, they showered on their principals with the fine generosity of children dispensing make-believe coin. Balzac was one of the first to undertake careful calculations, to mete out exactly what he thought his characters should have, and to cause the action of a story—as in *Père Goriot*—to turn on money or the lack of it. *The Way of All Flesh* brought a respect for money into English fiction, condemning Ernest's inability to handle it as one of his chief weaknesses. *Buddenbrooks* is still more explicit about the size of the family fortune, the various losses it suffers through marriage settlements and bad speculations. Because this is a commercial family, the state of its fortune serves as an index to its general state. When its possessions decline, its morale and its very hold on existence likewise deteriorate. Even the crimes which affect its standing are commercial crimes, the bankruptcy of Tony's husband, the embezzlement of her son-in-law.

In portraying his characters Mann has, for the most part, been content with classical methods. There is no attempt to limit the point of view, which shifts easily from one to another, though it is always given to some member of the family. Nor is there much stress on that exploring of the unconscious which recent psychological developments have brought so strongly to the fore, and which plays so large a part in *The Magic Mountain*.

The restraint which makes Mann's literary devices almost imperceptible is admirably illustrated in the case of Tom Buddenbrook, who is revealed as much through behavioristic as through analytical detail. His "Buddenbrook hand," and his death have been mentioned as examples of realism and symbolism. The modification of the hand may be taken to indicate the suppressed artistic impulses hinted at in his choice of a wife and openly expressed in his son. The strange deterioration which takes place within him so that he feels himself eaten away by a species of spiritual dry rot, is revealed through his growing obsession with details of wardrobe and toilet. As the inner man melts away he strengthens his armor of spotless elegance, till in the end he is but the exquisite shell of a man. Here Mann achieves a realistic and far more effective treatment of the theme which Henry James played upon more crudely and more fantastically in *The Private Life*.

The character of Tom is effective, just as the general technique of *Buddenbrooks* is effective, because it hovers on the border line between two types, and benefits by both. Apparently normal, he yet suffers from conflicts and suppressions which play a large part in abnormal psychology. One feels that he is straining against the bars which hold him to stolid decorum, and this sense of stress increases the poignancy of his characterization. The distance he has traveled between self-confident young manhood and his final state, is well brought out by two scenes which also illustrate Mann's masterful economy: the first, Tom's interview with his mistress, the little florist's assistant,

when moved, but very much master of himself, he bids
her a final good-by; the second, his suffering as he sits
alone in his office listening to his wife and the handsome
lieutenant making music in a room above—a prey to sus-
picions of a spiritual betrayal far more torturing than
those based on physical infidelity.

Tom's evolution from assured and almost callous con-
servatism to anguished sensitivity is counter-balanced by
that of Tony, who changes from an impetuous young
girl into the spirit of conventionality and the personifica-
tion of the family point of view. Her very conversation
grows to be a compote of *clichés* in which the jargon of
the Forty-eighters, sole vestige of her youthful revolt,
clashes oddly with the bromides of the seventies and
eighties, by which she shapes her life.

The family deterioration, recapitulated in Tom's character, takes final form in Hanno's physical weakness and
artistic temperament. His tooth troubles, described with
extreme realism, also serve as a symbol of general debility;
and that his weakness stems directly from his father is
emphasized by the fact that it is a decayed tooth which
precipitates Tom's death. In addition, the teeth offer
opportunity for implied comment on the rôle of dentistry
in modern life, and the essential impotence of dentists,
doctors, and all the agents of science to exercise that help-

ful control which is supposed to be their function. As for the aesthetic leanings suppressed in Tom and evident in Hanno, they too become symbols of decadence since they are wholly at odds with the sturdy commercialism which is the essence of the Buddenbrooks. The genius of the family has been the sort that could be reflected through rooms shining with comfort and cleanliness, opulent fur coats, and superabundance of good things to eat. When it descends to such a vessel as a frail, tearful boy with bad teeth, a weak digestion, and a burning love for music, it has declined indeed!

Because the point of view is limited to the family which is the group hero, the real touch of caricature is reserved for outsiders, such as Tony's second husband, Herr Permaneder from Munich, who is sketched with something of the good natured satire turned upon those beyond the pale. The Buddenbrooks are always sympathetically portrayed. Yet irony is never far from the surface, though so suavely insinuated that the reader feels it his own, developed from a strictly realistic representation of the material. Herein lies Mann's triumph. *Buddenbrooks* seems to take seriously the family and the family ideals; it almost does so. Nevertheless, by methods more veiled than innuendo, it does imply a satirical comment on pride of family, on provincial, and even national pride. One suspects, even though it is not hinted, that Tom's later preoccupation with clothes is a sly dig at the last Kaiser.

The irony strikes deeper, however, down to the very roots of human aspiration, both worldly and other-worldly. Its full force is for an instant released during Tom's one moment of vision, which gives the most elo-quent passage in the book, and which by implication adds to the painfulness of his death when at last it comes. Dipping into a stray treatise on philosophy he seems to find an inkling of the strength he needs, and an assurance of some deeper portent in life itself. The assurance grows as he thinks it over during the night:

✶

"I shall live!" said Thomas Buddenbrook, almost aloud, and felt his breast shaken with inward sobs. "This is the revelation; that I shall live." . . . He wept, he pressed his face into the pillows and wept, shaken through and through, lifted up in transports by a joy without com-pare. . . .

. . . He never succeeded in looking again into the precious volume—to say nothing of buying its other parts. His days were consumed by nervous pedantry: harassed by a thousand details, all of them unimportant, he was too weak-willed to arrive at a reasonable and fruitful arrangement of his time. Nearly two weeks after that memorable afternoon he gave it up—and ordered the maidservant to fetch the book from the drawer in the garden table and replace it in the bookcase.

✕

This might be, as it purports to be, merely an account of what happens. Yet it carries overtones of comment on Tom and his species as well as on the value of mystical assurances concerning the life everlasting. A similar chord is struck in the very last scene. The Buddenbrook women on the eve of the family's final disintegration, meet in a pathetic conclave that recalls by contrast the buoyant group with which the novel began. There are quiet tears but there is also courage; and Tony in a moment of exaltation asks whether there can be an after life in which may occur a joyous reunion of Buddenbrooks. Her kinswomen are silent—this is not their field. But Sesemi Weichbrodt, Tony's old teacher and the family's staunch friend, undertakes to answer:

✕

"*It is so!*" she said, with her whole strength; and looked at them all with a challenge in her eyes.

She stood there, a victor in the good fight which all her life she had waged against the assaults of Reason: humpbacked, tiny, quivering with the strength of her con-

95

victions, a little prophetess, admonishing and inspired.

✗

Does Thomas Mann see Sesemi as sublime or ridicu-
lous, or a little of both? The essence of his art lies in
leaving the question open.

✗

SEVEN

BOSTON

T HE novel of purpose, here represented by Upton Sinclair's *Boston*, has enjoyed a long and highly respectable career, especially in England where it is well suited to the general tradition of moral and didactic fiction. It rose to great prominence in the eighteenth century, inspired by Rousseau's doctrine of individualism and the natural man. Its two main types at this time were the educational novel, represented in France by Rousseau's *Emile* and in England by Thomas Day's *Sandford and Merton,* and the political novel, such as William Godwin's *Caleb Williams,* wherein he illustrated the findings of his *Enquiry Concerning Political Justice,* and denounced the evil effects of power alike upon its possessors and its victims.

The nineteenth century, with its growing consciousness of inter-class friction, produced numbers of novels frankly written to expound the author's social theories. Disraeli in *Sybil,* Charles Kingsley in *Yeast* and *Alton Locke,*

characters, a tinge of the English sporting gentleman's condescending gratitude to the faithful retainers who make possible his daily bath, his well browned mutton, and his sacred Derby.

There are instances, however, where this throwback is eliminated, and members of the privileged classes are seen as straining with an eagerness almost mystical to identify themselves with the masses. This is the spirit of Tolstoy, of William Morris, and also of Upton Sinclair. In *Boston* his chief character, Cornelia Thornwell, does not stoop from on high as Lady Bountiful. She has no idea of philanthropy, a motive which Tolstoy discredited once for all. Her desire is to be a working woman. Sinclair is realistic enough to make her fail in that aim. But at least she does succeed in being a friend of the working people, and in identifying her interests with theirs. She is the dramatic expression of William Morris's thesis:

✖

We well-to-do people . . . have for our best work the raising of the standard of life among the people. How can we of the middle classes, we the capitalists and our hangers-on, help? By renouncing our class, and on all occasions when antagonism rises up between the classes, casting in our lot with the victims; those who are condemned at the best to lack of education, refinement, leisure,

100

pleasure and renown; and at the worst, to a life lower than that of the most brutal savages. There is no other way.

✗

Galsworthy, who has devoted a large proportion of his fiction to a study of class relations, has brought out perhaps even more clearly than Sinclair the difficulty of what Cornelia wished to achieve—the subtle impregnability of the barriers, some of them physical, which help to make of the rich and poor two separate nations. As he shows in *Fraternity,* habits of cleanliness, even the sense of smell, tend to divide humanity into classes. According to his wont, Galsworthy recognizes these difficulties with regret rather than condemnation. Tolstoy's attitude toward the situation was more protestant:

✗

Without prejudice I looked into our own mode of life, and became aware that it was not by chance that closer intercourse with the poor is difficult for us, but that we ourselves are intentionally ordering our lives in such a way as to make this intercourse impossible. And not only this; but, on looking at our lives, or at the lives of rich people, from without, I saw that all that is considered as the *summum bonum* of these lives consists in being separated as much as possible from the poor, or is in some way or other connected with this desired separation.

In fact, all the aim of our lives, beginning with food,

101

dress, dwelling, cleanliness, and ending with our education, consists in placing a gulf between us and them. And
in order to establish this distinction and separation we
spend nine-tenths of our wealth in erecting impassable
barriers.

✗

The novel of purpose, dedicated to propaganda and
based upon journalistic fact, is almost by definition limited in its artistry. A certain amount of pamphlet material must be interspersed with the fiction, and as a rule
the author is too much imbued with his thesis to subordinate it to the interests of his art. In this respect,
however, *Boston,* based on the Sacco-Vanzetti case, com-
pares favorably with its predecessors of the eighteenth and
nineteenth centuries, and also with the previous works
of its author.

Upton Sinclair is a Southerner by inheritance, an
ascetic by reaction, a romantic by temperament. His
parents experienced the miseries of life in the South after
the Civil War, and misfortune followed them, even after
their final establishment in New York. These early
troubles, not the least of which was his father's addiction
to drink, had their share in developing the revolutionary
attitude which marked Sinclair as a youthful poet and
as a mature, though still youthful, novelist. He, like

Flaubert, combines the dual strain of realist and romanticist; but the conflict from which Flaubert suffered is minimized in the case of Sinclair, who finds his material adequate to both impulses. Whereas Flaubert's romanticism demanded distant climes and times, Sinclair's finds its outlet in the fervor of the idealism he brings to bear upon the here and now. Flaubert turned upon ancient Carthage the hard dry light of realism; Sinclair suffuses modern Babylon with the purple glow of romance which transfigures, not the facts he so mercilessly exposes, but the rebels whose opposition to injustice represents society's sole alleviation and hope.

The Jungle (1905) in which Sinclair uncovered the shocking conditions of the Chicago stockyards, is the book which made his reputation, not only in America but also abroad, where he is even today our best known novelist. It has been followed by numerous volumes, both journalism and fiction. In each case his object was to expose some current evil, and in each case the author's contentions are backed by a formidable amount of documentation. *Boston,* like *Oil* which preceded and *Mountain City* which followed it, shows Sinclair at his best, welding the material of his researches into a story which is interesting in itself.

One reason for the greater success of *Boston* in sub-

103

duing journalistic material to novel form was that in this case Sinclair found his facts already reduced to terms of human interest. In *The Jungle* he created a lay fig-- ure—a Lithuanian peasant—to dramatize the situation he wished to discuss. But in Sacco and Vanzetti, society offered him two individuals expressly designed to personify the struggle. Thus, *The Jungle* starts with certain general conditions dramatized through characters obviously concocted for purposes of demonstration; while *Boston* grew out of an intense human drama, obviously chosen because it demonstrates certain general conditions. Such material furnishes the best possible safeguard against subordinating characters to propaganda.

To the type of mind which chooses to write novels of purpose—that is, one interested in social rather than in personal problems—artistic considerations must be secondary. *Boston* is fifty per cent pamphlet. The story proper cannot be called entirely fiction, since many of its characters are based on life, and some carry their actual names. The account of the proceedings is based on written records and personal interviews. The very gossip which the characters retail has been drawn from weeks spent listening to the intimate chit-chat of Bostonians, often concerning living persons. In this mingling of actual and fictitious characters Sinclair has brought the his-

104

torical novel up to date, and created a new form of realism.

Compared to so well carpentered a novel as *Budden-brooks*, *Boston* appears almost amorphous in structure; the work of a man who commands the resources of an artist, but who prefers—as so many novelists of purpose have preferred—to subordinate those powers to the cause he pleads. This preference appears unfortunate from the forensic as well as the aesthetic point of view. One suspects that the patently biased comment of the author weakens rather than strengthens his case, and that greater artfulness in presenting the facts might have brought the disinterested or disaffected reader into more active sympathy with his viewpoint.

Sinclair, however, has renounced subtle means in favor of the simplest possible scheme for covering the salient angles of his case. Just as a good city editor manages to post a reporter wherever the story is apt to "break," so Sinclair, himself a journalist par excellence, has openly plotted out his characters for the purpose of supplying actions and reactions typical of as many points of view as possible. He has been particularly successful in his principal character, "The Runaway Grandmother," who represents the aristocracy's revolt against itself and in favor of the proletariat. Although drawn from life, Cornelia Thornwell furnishes the fictional hub of the book.

Technically, its plot is an account of her attempt to withdraw from the meretricious physical and mental sloth of her group and identify herself with those who, she feels, live closer to realities. For this purpose she leaves her aristocratic family and takes lodgings in a poor Italian home where Vanzetti is also a lodger. It is through this coincidence that her story becomes identified with his; the trial, imprisonment, and execution of Sacco and Vanzetti are crucial elements in forming her final conclusions. Thus Sinclair gains fictional justification for making *Boston* the story of the Sacco-Vanzetti trial.

Cornelia is in an excellent position to serve as spokeswoman, or *raisonneuse*, throughout the book; so excellent, in fact, that the author might have entrusted his comment entirely to her, instead of speaking so often in his own person. She is qualified to contrast the manners, interests, ideals, of rich and poor, and to deliver his verdict on the comparison. Since he is an idealist, that verdict differs radically from the pragmatic and rather cynical views of Butler and his literary descendants. In *The Way of All Flesh* Butler treats the idea that the poor are superior to the rich as a sentimental superstition, and greets Ernest's denial of it as one step in his march toward intellectual validity. Sinclair, on the other hand, really believes that by virtue of their training, the poor are better than the rich. One basis of his belief, enunciated by Cornelia, emphasizes in this sense the class differences noted by Tolstoy and Galsworthy:

✕

"Remember," she tells her son-in-law, "I saw Vanzetti carry a half-conscious man off the picket-line, I sat by while he bathed the broken head, I saw him weeping, I heard him babbling like a child, incoherent, hysterical, with mingled grief and rage. He has that temperament, he suffers more than either you or I do—he cares—that is the difference, he really cares! You and I care whether we have dinner in proper style, whether the Madeira is real or not, whether the lobster was alive or not, whether the chicken is the right age and the salad dressing sufficiently solid, whether we have got on the right costume and the right tie, whether we hold our knives and forks the right way, whether we make a sufficient display of worldly cynicism, whether we are sufficiently skeptical about all enthusiasms, sufficiently dead to faith, hope and charity."

✕

Cornelia's associations with capitalism justify the inclusion of other actual cases. One of these is that of the management of the New York, New Haven and Hartford Railroad, under the domination of J. P. Morgan. The other, represented in the book by Jerry Walker and his felt factory, is the Willett case in which a group of

107

Boston lawyers and bankers were found to have used their financial power to ruin an independent business man. Sinclair makes skillful use of this opportunity to contrast the law which governs the rich with that which governs the poor. Here, as in reporting the Sacco-Vanzetti case, he has kept strictly to fact supported by the records of government investigations or judicial proceedings.

The sincerity of his attempt to keep within the factual truth has been questioned with regard to his portraits of Sacco and Vanzetti. But here, too, all claims are well documented. Their letters quoted in *Boston,* are among those which appeared in the collected letters of the two men published in 1928. When this volume came out it was assumed by certain English reviews that they were forged. The supposition, though understandable in view of the rather bewildering eloquence displayed by two humble immigrants, is easily disproved. Both men became cultivated during their years of imprisonment. Neither perfected his English, but the long drawn out suffering of the experience combined with their initial temperaments, resulted in giving to each a style and a point of view which partake of grandeur. Nothing in *Boston* is more powerful than the contrast of two authentic documents. The first, the will of Judge Elbert H. Gary, head of the United States Steel Corporation:

"I earnestly request my wife and children and descendants that they steadfastly decline to sign any bonds or obligations of any kind as surety for any other person, or persons; that they refuse to make any loans except on the basis of first-class, well-known securities, and that they invariably decline to invest in any untried or doubtful securities of property or enterprise or business."

✕

The second is from Sacco's last letter to his son:

✕

"So, son, instead of crying, be strong, so as to be able to comfort your mother, and when you want to distract your mother from the discouraging soulness, I will tell you what I used to do. To take her for a long walk in the quiet country, gathering wild flowers here and there, resting under the shade of trees, between the harmony of the vivid stream and the gentle tranquillity of the mother nature, and I am sure that she will enjoy this very much, as you surely would be happy for it. But remember always, Dante, in the play of happiness, don't you use all for yourself only, but down yourself just one step, at your side and help the weak ones that cry for help, help the persecuted and the victim because they are your better friends, they are the comrades that fight and fall as your father and Bartolo fought and fell yesterday for the conquest of the joy and freedom for all the poor workers. In this struggle of life you will find more love and you will be loved."

From their letters it is clear that, considered in the light of spiritual values, the victims gained by their martyrdom; that they were finer individuals and better citizens because of it. Vanzetti, at least, realized and declared this fact. The question put and answered by *Boston* is whether society in general and Massachusetts justice in particular can afford to enrich members of the community by such methods.

Mr. W. G. Thompson, once head of the Suffolk County Bar and eventually chief counsel for the defense, thought it could not. He is one of the characters who appear under their own names. The views which he enunciates in *Boston* are those which he himself expressed; but also, they serve to express the ideas of the author, and in a manner the more forceful because they issue from a man who up to that time had been a successful and conservative lawyer. Sinclair realizes that his own prejudices are suspect, since he began with a frank socialistic bias; whereas it was Thompson's very reverence for the established law which caused him to investigate charges that it was being unfairly administered—and when he found those charges true, to put his whole effort into an attempt to right the wrong. Thus he, like Cornelia, speaks with an accent more convincing than Sinclair's own, when he says:

110

"Every Federal agent who knew anything about it believed these men to be innocent of murder. 'Every one of us believed they ought to be deported. They were anarchists, they did not believe in organized government or private property.' [Here Thompson was quoting the statement of two Federal agents.] Oh, how those words will ring around this world, 'private property!' Think what is going to be said about it! The man who does not believe in private property in America may be killed whether he is guilty or not. That is going to be said from one end of the world to the other if this thing is allowed to go through. Can we afford it?"

✕

The idea of private property is naturally one of the centers on which the whole book turns. Through the Jerry Walker case, the theories of Vanzetti, the expressions of Thompson, Cornelia, and other characters, Sinclair manages to bring out the pros and cons of the question quite thoroughly. That it is an international question is stressed by the fact that in this instance its agitators were Italians in America, and the feeling against them was based on their suspected relations with revolutionary parties abroad, a recrudescence of the old hatred of the foreigner by the native son which found political expression in the Know Nothing Party of the Forties, and the Hundred Per Cent Americanism after the World War. But

111

aside from this, *Boston* is distinctly American in the picture of life it presents, in the angles from which it considers its chosen problems, in the spirit which informs—and forms—the whole. The Boston capitalists, despite their lineage, are a different race from Galsworthy's Forsytes; the life in Boston moves to a different tempo from the tranquil tread in Mann's Lübeck. In reporting one of the most characteristic, if most unfortunate, episodes of twentieth century American history, Sinclair has captured for all time the flavor of American urban life in the third decade of the twentieth century.

His picture, his principles, indeed the whole tenor of the book, may easily prove irritating to the reader. This is a necessary feature of a book written to plead a cause: its opponents will be annoyed by its thesis, quite aside from the manner of its presentation. But whatever the reaction to the doctrine it sets forth, no one can doubt the eloquence of the plea, nor the force with which the rudimentary technique is employed. Nor can one doubt that this book, half novel, half pamphlet, takes its place as an important example of a novelistic type which has played a significant part in the past, and doubtless will continue to do so in the future.

THE POST-REALISTIC NOVEL

THE development of the novel has been a constant striving toward realization, through the written word, of the great experience all human beings share in common—the experience of being alive. In that sense, every change introduced since the art of fiction began to take itself seriously might have been termed realism, since each was prompted by the desire to come closer to the author's conception of the truth about life. That conception, however individual, would inevitably reflect the beliefs of his time. Because our idea of reality has altered, realism today is totally different from the ideal held by its first disciples. Modern realists have abandoned the search for objective truth, condemning the very attempt to be objective as unrealistic. This attitude is a direct result of recent findings in anthropology, psychology, history, and the physical sciences.

Science influences modern fiction as forcefully through the concepts it has destroyed as by those it has built up.

Much has been written and more has been said, concerning the breakdown of old values and the gap they have left in our living and thinking. Belief in an after life, idealization of romantic love, the immutability of moral standards, the grandeur of death, the dependability of facts, have crumbled under a growing inclination to view religion as superstition, love as biology, morality as *mores,* death as ignominy, and any knowledge we may possess as fragmentary, tentative, relative.

Having lost, through science, the "lendings" which conferred upon life its dignity and meaning, we have transferred our attention to the substitute favored by science—life itself, as glimpsed within the individual. Researches in psychology, particularly in psycho-analysis, have encouraged this shift, bestowing upon fiction a new set of concepts and of labels for them. D. H. Lawrence and May Sinclair furnish examples of psycho-analytic theory directly applied, but they are merely representative of a whole group who have abandoned the outer for the inner drama. One result of psychological research clearly evident in contemporary fiction, is a broadening of "normality" to include what would once have been rejected as incongruous or pathological. Early novelists avoided making their characters seem inconsistent. Today, an appreciation of the conflicting impulses which render each individual a complex of personalities rather than a consistent unit, is vital to any sense of reality. The Russians anticipated us in admitting incongruity of characterization, because, as suggested in the chapter on *Anna Karénina*, they were less bound than we by set formulae and accepted patterns. But the enthusiasm with which we follow their lead grows from the change in our own attitude.

In an effort to communicate most cogently the experience of being alive, the author has tended more and more to adopt the viewpoint of the characters he is portraying. Formerly, analysis of mental states and processes was offered as by a separate and omniscient entity. Gradually the barrier between writer and protagonist has been lowered, till now we find the protagonist's inner consciousness turned out to view and speaking for itself in monologue without quotation marks.

This "stream-of-consciousness" technique is most consistently applied by Dorothy Richardson, who, in her *Pilgrimage*, a series of novels now numbering nine, tells only what Miriam perceives, and as she perceives it. The result is a heightened vividness, and also a certain confusion. Information which a nineteenth century novelist would have retailed in orderly sequence is grasped piecemeal, and often understood only after several refer-

115

ences or even several readings. Trivial details are stressed as in life, without the conventional selection of what is "relevant to the story." What the reader is to retain is not the chronicle of a life, but the sense of a person, known, not as we know our friends, but as we know ourselves—with deeper insight, less perspective, and no presumption of a finality which because it is unrealizable, is unrealistic.

James Joyce in *Ulysses* has been less extreme than Miss Richardson in limiting point of view. He speaks through three characters, alternating from one to the other, and occasionally taking liberties which remind us that there is an interpreter behind the personality on display. He has, however, pushed the representation of mental processes further than any contemporary, drafting the methods of music and poetry into the service of realism, and with the methods, the prerogative of demanding effortful study. In a subsequent work not yet published in full, Joyce carries his explorations through the borderland of sleep. Here he limits himself to a single consciousness.

Ulysses is one of our least read and most discussed books.

It begins with Stephen Dedalus, carried over from the earlier autobiographical novel *Portrait of the Artist as a Young Man* and still identifiable as Joyce. After picturing Stephen's unsatisfactory life and hinting at his background—always through the medium of his own consciousness—the scene shifts to Leopold Bloom, an intelligent though uncultivated Dublin Jew whose wife is known by all his world, including himself, to be unfaithful. Twice during the day the paths of these two intersect, but not until evening do they really come together. Bloom invites Stephen to live in his home, and though Stephen refuses, the episode rehabilitates them both—Bloom in his own estimation and that of his wife, Stephen in his resolve to pursue his work of writing. This is but the baldest sketch of the narrative buried in long passages of revery interspersed with dialogue; passages bewildering for readers accustomed to the aid of paragraphing and punctuation. Here ideas, sentences, words, are mangled, distorted, telescoped, in an attempt to reproduce the mental shorthand each person uses toward himself, and to make its rhythm, imagery, vocabulary, representative of the user. The thing that is actually happening, the past it recalls, the meditation it provokes, jostle, interrupt, obscure each other. Yet behind the confusion dwells a steady purpose, which Edmund Wilson in his illuminating critique of Joyce has summed up as the desire:

117

. . . . to render as accurately as it is possible in words to do, what our participation in life is like—or rather, what it seems to us like as from moment to moment we live.

✖

Regarding the success of this endeavor, Mr. Wilson says:

✖

The trouble has really been that the first readers of *Ulysses* were shocked by the way in which the incongruous elements of our complex human organism were mingled in Joyce's characters—or rather, by the way in which Joyce has violated the traditional conventions for representing the mingling of these elements. But the more we read *Ulysses,* the more we feel its psychological truth, and the more we are astonished by Joyce's genius in grasping, not through analysis or generalization, but by the direct representation of life in the process of being lived, the relations of human beings to their environment and to each other, the nature of their perception of what goes on about them and of what goes on within themselves, and the interdependence of their intellectual, their physical, their professional, and their emotional lives. To have traced all these interdependences, to have given each of these elements its value, yet never to have lost sight of the moral through the physical, nor to have forgotten the general in the particular; to have presented us with ordinary humanity without either satirizing or sentimentalizing it—this would already have been sufficiently remarkable; but to have turned such material into poetry, and that poetry of the highest order, is a feat which has hardly been equaled in English in our age.

✕

Thus the book itself illustrates the relativism which is so large a part of Joyce's message and of current thought. From one point of view, and one which claims respectable backing, *Ulysses* appears but a welter of of coagulated syllables. Differently approached, it may yield a wealth of beauty and of understanding which repays all the labor of extracting it.

This labor is two-fold. Any intelligent, or at least, any intellectual reader, may hope to fathom the vocabulary and reclaim the sunken narrative. But the symbolism remains. As the title indicates, the novel is patterned after Homer's epic. Not only do the three chief characters correspond to Ulysses, Penelope, and Telemachus, but each incident, even the slightest, parallels some episode in the Odyssey. Moreover, each section symbolizes some human organ and some art or science. The writing is designed for the symbolism as well as the story, and the two are not always identical. A character is arbitrarily forced into meditations which permit a vocabulary related to the symbol, which may be further suggested by fantastic word-play, parody, or a subtler effect that might be called onomatopoeia of style. Thus at any moment, in addition to persons themselves both realistic and symbolic, there are present two sets of symbols, treated with a piquant melange of literal and allusive representation. This esoteric quality is typical of much contemporary writing, which is more concerned, as Middleton Murry has said, with discovering the truth than with communicating it.

Another respect in which *Ulysses* is typical, is that despite prodigious length, the pilgrimage of Stephen Dedalus (Telemachus) in search of his spiritual father, Bloom (Ulysses) is kept within the span of one day. This spreading of little time over many pages is inevitable to exhaustive analysis of consciousness. Virginia Woolf's *Mrs. Dalloway,* another example of realism verging on poetry, also takes place within one day, and many others find two hundred pages insufficient for the chronicle of twenty-four hours. Of Marcel Proust, a character in recent fiction observes that he is the man who devotes a whole volume to the flicker of an eyelid.

There is more justice in this remark concerning an author who shares the importance of Joyce, than in the fact that he also shares Joyce's reputation for unreadability. Proust is not difficult in the manner of Joyce. It is true his sentences are extremely long, somewhat involved, and burdened by a mass of metaphor which would be florid were it not so invariably exact. His vocabulary and syntax are orthodox, however, and though his work is also constructed after an elaborate plan, comprehension of it does not involve acquaintance with a "program" outside the book itself. After reading the seven double volumes of *A La Recherche du Temps Perdu* one is in a position to appreciate the structure of this literary symphony, which introduces in the very first volume every theme and every character to be developed. Merely by reading, one comes to discern purpose in the apparently haphazard scheme which devotes a hundred and fifty pages to a dinner party, but drops out whole years of the principal character's transition from childhood to middle age, and instead of pursuing a straight chronological course, tacks in time like a novel by Conrad.

It is appropriate to speak first of time in discussing Proust, since as Clive Bell puts it, time is the hero of his masterpiece, with the unconscious for heroine. Proust does not, however, reveal the unconscious through the stream-of-consciousness technique, but writes frankly in the first person. Edwin Muir has described *A La*

121

Recherche du Temps Perdu as several character and dramatic novels, combining to form another novel. This enclosing frame is in one sense a thesis novel, although its tenets are aesthetic rather than social, and its aim is to demonstrate rather than to preach. Proust contends that the only book worth writing is the one dictated to the author by his own life. Proust shared Flaubert's belief that a man can know only himself; but it led him to the opposite conclusion. Instead of trying to eliminate himself from his writing, he wrote only about himself, or about others as sensed by him.

The frame novel concerns the narrator, who may with certain reservations be identified with the author. (The whole is to a great extent autobiographical, yet every person, every thing, almost every incident described, is a composite rather than a direct adoption from life.) The narrator's history, like that of Ulysses, is a psychological pilgrimage. Starting from the idealism represented by his adored grandmother, the boy allured by false gods spends his energies in a life of frivolity and unsatisfactory amours. But in a final scene, analogous to religious conversion, he determines to renounce Vanity Fair and, like Stephen Dedalus, to devote the remainder of his life to literature—thus reverting to the idealism represented by his early environment. There is a distinct moral in these two accounts of an errant individual returning to what constitutes for him the good life—i. e. fighting through frustration to adjustment. But because aesthetic principles and individual integrity have been substituted for the religious or moral values hitherto associated with reform, that aspect of the two books is not generally recognized.

The account of Proust's "narrator"—one so unsparingly portrayed could hardly be called hero—involves minor stories, such as the exquisite metropolitan idyll called "Swann in Love," and the less normal relationships of the narrator with Albertine, and the Baron de Charlus with a violinist named Morel. The various social groups he penetrates are described and satirized with a touch that varies from delicate miniature work to broad caricature. As in *Ulysses*, external event merely provides the point of departure. Nevertheless, in both cases, people and scenes assume a reality both dramatic and psychological. They live. The two books employ strikingly different means to achieve this three-, or rather four-dimensional actuality in the worlds they create, and in each, the technique may be explained partly through the author's physical handicap. Because Joyce has always suffered from defective eyesight, his responses are audial rather than visual. His description, character portrayal, the very ingenuity of his style, bespeak one who is word-minded. Proust was from early childhood a victim of asthma and an affection of the nerves, which kept him a recluse for many years, heightening his powers of perception and introspection to a morbid degree. Partly, at least, in consequence, he describes the most minute effects with a completeness unprecedented in literature; and his analysis is equally probing, equally accurate, equally exhaustive, for the physical and the psychological. Like Joyce, he also illustrates the surge of erudition into modern fiction. Both authors are (in both senses of the word) possessed of an impressive culture, which forms an integral part of the work of each. There is an essay to be written on the importance of book learning in fiction today, but present space limits permit only the observation that it is there.

Unlike the stream-of-consciousness novelists, who picture life unfolding from moment to moment, Proust tells his whole story through the perspective of memory. Reminiscence begins and ends his work, furnishes the lens through which his narrative is focussed, and brings to the narrator his keenest joy, his deepest understanding, his final decision to write. Yet memory only serves to define the general theories about truth, time and man which caused *A La Recherche du Temps Perdu* to be hailed—with approximate accuracy though much to Proust's disgust—as a Bergsonian novel. It not only dramatizes the precepts of the French philosopher, but also puts the principles of relativity into human terms. Proust has tried to depict the eternal flux and change of human relationships and human character, portraying each individual as a series of personalities linked in a chain of experience and varying according to the time and the mood of himself and his associates. His whole novel is an enlargement of the definition of man given by one of Einstein's chief interpreters: a four-dimensional worm, the fourth dimension being time. Through this presentation, Proust has attempted to capture the essence of reality; not the truth about each individual, since that is a variable, but the constant laws, the "eternal verities," which the artist distills from experience. He has approached these eternal verities largely through memory, believing that only in retrospect does truth emerge.

This endeavor to delve past appearance into meanings, is one element connecting Proust with the English rather than the French tradition. By an exchange of lineage which nicely emphasizes how art reflects our growing internationalism, Joyce figures in the French line of descent. He, too, suggests the universal, but only through complete portrayal of the particular. True to naturalistic theory, he generalizes by implication only, giving no clue to his purpose and belief save that inherent in the minds and deeds of his characters. Proust, on the other hand, bares his motives, declares his notions of literature and of life, and openly points to the way his characters demonstrate them.

Here is more than a difference in method. Proust's very belief in eternal verities and ultimate truths runs counter to the prevailing acceptance of all truth, whether spiritual or physical, as relative. It is an enlightening contradiction to find this mystical certainty underlying a work in other respects so typical of its period. For explanation one must look to the personality and Hebraic heritage of the man himself. He was fortunate, however, to have faith in a day when most novelists are crying with Flaubert, *"je suis mystique et au fond je ne crois à rien."*

Both Proust and Joyce have been blamed for dealing with unpleasant material, and both answer the reproach with scorn. Proust, however, adds argument to his contempt, pointing out in his last volume that only through study of the abnormal may truth about normality be grasped, and that for any understanding of people and of life it is necessary to realize how much of the normal the abnormal includes, and vice versa. Only through a complete portrayal of life could he achieve what he held to be the two-fold purpose of art: to offer his audience escape through participation in the unique universe inhabited by each original artist, and at the same time to hold out "an optical instrument whereby the reader may more truly see himself."

In their differences no less than their similarities, these two writers epitomize the chief development of current fiction. The aim of that development is realistic, but it seeks a psychological rather than a physical realism. It recognizes the experience of being alive as the most interesting, most unifying, most essential of human adventures; it stresses both the diversity and the similarity of conscious and unconscious processes. In the light of all that has been learned through science and through art, it attempts to reproduce with the greatest possible fidelity what Proust said *"ought to be most precious and normally remains forever unknown, our true life, reality as we have felt it."*

✕